BOSH!

SIMPLE RECIPES

AMAZING FOOD

ALL PLANTS

BOSH!

HENRY FIRTH & IAN THEASBY

H|Q

ook is dedicated to you, whoever and
ver you are. We hope this book pleases
lights you, and takes you on a journey.

 of HarperCollins*Publishers* Ltd
Bridge Street
1 9GF

hed in Great Britain by HQ
 of HarperCollins*Publishers* Ltd 2018

ight © Henry Firth and Ian Theasby 2018

hy Copyright © Lizzie Mayson 2018

 and Ian Theasby assert the moral right to be identified as
s of this work. A catalogue record for this book is available
ritish Library.

)-00-826290-7

 is to use papers that are natural, renewable and
 products and made from wood grown in sustainable
e logging and manufacturing processes conform to
nvironmental regulations of the country of origin.

nformation visit: www.harpercollins.co.uk/green

hy: Lizzie Mayson
g: Pip Spence
g: Sarah Birks
rt Direction: Paul Palmer-Edwards, GradeDesign.com
mmissioning Editor: Rachel Kenny
tor: Sarah Hammond
esign: Louise McGrory

 bound in Great Britain by Bell & Bain Ltd, Glasgow

MIX

Contents

Welcome

We're here to show you how you can eat delightful meals that are both easy to cook and incredibly satisfying, all using just plants.

Let us introduce you to a new way of thinking about food; one that we've developed and perfected together over the last three years, and that is becoming increasingly popular.

It involves eating delicious, hearty, even indulgent meals that are both comfortingly familiar and exciting, and without any need for meat or dairy.

It's also a new way of cooking. Animal products are so ingrained in the human diet that we've had tens of thousands of years to hone the art of cooking with them. But the concept of cooking without meat and dairy is still relatively new. Which can only mean one thing: there is so much potential yet to be unleashed from plant-based eating.

We promise you'll find in this book your new, fail-safe family favourites, inspiring lunch ideas, showstoppers that'll impress even the most staunch steak-lover, tasty snacks, outrageously good puds (we're pretty good at those, if we do say so ourselves) and awesome cocktails, every one bursting with flavour.

So, whether you're thinking about reducing the amount of meat you eat, or you don't eat animal products at all, this book is for you.

BOSH!

If you'd told us three years ago we were going to spend our lives cooking and eating amazing plant-based food, we wouldn't have believed you. We were a couple of mates from Sheffield who ate meat every single week.

Now we run BOSH!, the biggest plant-based online channel in the world. Our food creations were viewed by half a billion people in our first year and our most popular recipe videos have been viewed over 50 million times. We never expected to have that kind of success, and it has been humbling.

'I was the one to first cut out animal products.'
Ian

'I mocked Ian when he went vegan, and asked him where he'd get his protein from. But eventually he won me over. That and the whole saving the world by not eating mass-produced animal products thing.'
Henry

After cutting out animal products entirely, both of us felt fantastic. But we had to re-learn how to cook and find food when we were out and about. We also found that the vegan food available in restaurants or in cookbooks was often, frankly, not very good.

We saw an opportunity. Since then, it's been our life's mission to show people how to make delicious plant-based meals. However often they choose to do that.

And now, after three years of eating plant-based food, we've mastered a new style of cooking, one made popular through a new breed of internet chefs, where novelty and wow-factor presentation are just as important as taste and ease.

With this new style of cooking, we've created all-plants versions of classic dishes that are free from meat, eggs and dairy, but still totally scrumptious. You know your favourite dishes, the ones you've learned by heart and use again and again? Well these are your new go-to classics.

Everything we do is aimed at showing just how easy it is to eat more plants. We also want to prove how delicious, hearty and satisfying plant-based food can be.

We cook, drink and film delicious recipes for the world, all from our home studio in East London.

x Henry and Ian

This book

Cook fast food fast. Spend time on showstoppers.
Sometimes you just need to eat quick, and you reach for your classic speedy dishes. Check out our Quick Eats chapter for yummy plates that you'll be able to get on the table in 30 minutes or less. Other times you're cooking for an occasion and looking to impress. Check out our Big Eats chapter for classics that will be worth the extra time, taking up to an hour to prep, or our Showpieces chapter for masterpieces that take that little bit longer (but the results are well worth it).

Get it right. First time. These are high-quality recipes.
Every recipe in this book has been rigorously and repeatedly tested again and again by us and our wonderful food team. We give you our word that these recipes work to a level that many in other cookbooks do not. These are high-quality recipes. Get the right kit, follow the instructions and you can easily cook these meals to perfection.

To make it easier for you to work quickly, we've also included the preparation instructions (like peeling and chopping) in the method. This ensures that you make the best use of your time, cooking as quickly as possible. We've also included a 'before you start' section above each recipe method, to highlight any special equipment you need or anything you should do before you start cooking. All oven temperatures are for fan ovens, so adjust the temperature if you have a conventional oven.

Create restaurant-quality meals at home
Check out our Fantastic Feasts section on page 17 to create menus as good as (or better than) anything you'll get from a restaurant or takeaway, with dishes that complement each other.

Whether you're in the mood for an Asian blowout, an Indian banquet, a Tex-Mex spread or a big Sunday lunch, you'll find everything you need in this book.

Watch videos to see how we do it
Looking for a helping hand when cooking a recipe? We've created a simple, top-down recipe video for the trickier dishes so you can see exactly how to cook them, step by step. Check out our website www.bosh.tv

Your kitchen

Here are a few tips from us to help you really master your kitchen and your cooking skills.

Be a continuously improving cook, whatever your level
Whether you're just starting out cooking only with plants or you're already accomplished with vegan food, there's always something new to learn. Here's how to be at the top of your game.

Treat each recipe you cook as an opportunity to learn something new. Don't fall into the trap of cooking the same things on repeat; find new recipes, get the right ingredients and try them out.

Up your skills from time to time with videos and books. Improve your knife skills with videos on YouTube. Use any of the amazing online tools, or a collection of cookbooks, to store up recipes to try in future. You can use post-its to mark the pages with recipes you want to try!

There's always something new to master, whether it's basics like getting vegan béchamel nailed or advanced baking with aquafaba. This new, plant-based way of thinking about food has so much freedom for innovation, so you'll be constantly improving.

Keep fruit and veggies on hand (or on ice) at all times!
A fridge full of fruit and veggies is not only good for your pocket, but they'll also keep really well. Onions, garlic and potatoes are best kept out of the fridge in a cool, dry place.

Got lots of fruit left over? Stick it in the freezer and use it to make morning smoothies. Peel and chop the fruit into bite-sized chunks and put it into a Tupperware container for easy use later. We have a constant store of frozen bananas, apples, berries, spinach, kale and watermelon ready to combine for a deliciously nutritious smoothie at any time of the day.

Bought too many veggies? That's OK: freeze them and use them later. Made too much pasta sauce? Pop it in a Tupperware or a freezer bag and keep it ready for a quick meal.

Keep your kitchen and pantry well organised to make life easier
Organise your pantry well and you'll always have meals ready to cook – check out page 15 for key ingredients to keep in stock. We go full nerd with sticky labels to highlight the right places for things. It makes cooking so much more satisfying and efficient because we're not constantly searching for ingredients in the cupboard.

We tend to organise our pantry shelves into sections like 'sauces & syrups', 'oils & vinegars', 'herbs & spices', 'flour, sugar & baking', 'grains, rice, pasta', plus the essential 'tea & coffee' shelf. Figure out a system that works for you. Trust us, knowing where things are makes fast cooking much easier.

Finally, organise your spices in a way that's easy to browse. We prefer smaller tubs of spices since they tend to be a consistent size and they usually have labels on the top. Plus, big bags of spice are harder to store and spices tend to go off if they're left on the shelf for too long. You'll soon discover which herbs and spices you get through quickly and which are worth buying in bulk – try decanting them into jars and adding your own labels on the lid.

EQUIPMENT

The equipment you find in your typical kitchen is going to work just fine for the recipes in this book. There is nothing super fancy or technical about what we do in our kitchen; we like to keep things simple. But, if we were going to design a cost-effective kitchen from scratch, here's how we would do it:

Essential items

These should be your go-to items. We use these every day to make great BOSH! food.

High-powered blender (like a NutriBullet, Magic Ninja or Magimix)

A **good, sharp knife** (and sharpener)

A selection of **chopping boards** that look great on the side and inspire you to cook

A **kitchen timer** or your mobile phone to get the timings right

Neatly stored spices, all in one place so you can find them quickly

A varied selection of preferably non-stick saucepans

Large spoons and tongs that work with your pans (don't use metal on non-stick!)

Measuring tools, like a measuring jug, weighing scales and measuring spoons

Nice-to-have items

Get these if you like. They will speed up your cooking, but they're optional.

Keep a clean **tea towel** in your pocket as you cook and you'll feel like a pro

Large-bowl **food processor** or **hand blender**

Oven-to-table dishes (for lasagne and pies)

Garlic crusher

A **grater** to zest or grate dairy-free cheese

A good **rolling pin**

Completely optional, but very cool items

These come in handy from time to time in our kitchen, so get them if you wish.

Pizza stone for better cooking and a crispier crust

Waffle iron

Toasted-sandwich maker

Slow cooker for long, slow, melt-in-the-mouth curries

Tiny dishes (soy sauce dishes) for measuring out spices before you start to cook

Sealing clips to keep opened packets of food from spilling everywhere

Tupperware or storage jars to keep your cupboards organised and store leftovers

Tofu press to make it even easier to cook with tofu

INGREDIENTS

The chances are that you already have most of these ingredients in your cupboard or your fridge. What we hope this book will do is unlock the potential in your store cupboard, and help you turn that humble tin of chickpeas into the most awesome falafel, or transform your usual pasta dish into something you'd be proud to serve at a dinner party. Get stocked up!

Essentials

If someone were to ask us what we keep in our kitchen cupboards, this would be the answer. We use these ingredients all the time and always keep them in stock so that we can whip up a quick meal without having to go to the shop first.

Pasta, in all its many forms, will answer your hunger prayers

Having **rice** in the cupboard means you'll always have something to eat

Noodles are a great base for speedy, nourishing and satisfying meals

Olive or groundnut oil, to use sparingly when frying or roasting

Sea salt and black pepper to season to perfection and bring your food to life

Garlic, because it's the best thing ever, used by nearly every cuisine in the world

Tinned chickpeas give you the wonder beans with which you can make hummus and falafel, plus aquafaba, an incredibly useful substitute for egg and dairy in cooking

Various tinned beans will ensure you get your protein whenever you need it

A stock of **tinned tomatoes** means you always have a base for sauces

A selection of spices for essential flavour – never underestimate their power

Fresh fruit, veggies and herbs because your mum told you to eat your greens and she was right

Nuts and seeds are fantastic for flavour, terrific for texture and super, super healthy

Peanut butter will give you energy, texture and flavour in abundance

Plant-based milk will crop up in our recipes again and again – we like almond milk best

Tinned coconut milk will help you craft creamy curries

Specialities

We tend to have these in our cupboards too, but we use them less frequently.

Nutritional yeast provides a nutty, cheesy taste and is a great source of vitamin B12

Cashew nuts can be soaked and blended for cream or cooked for a satisfying crunch

Passata will help your Italian dishes come to life

Kalamata olives add wonderful flavour and robust texture

Sun-dried tomatoes offer an incredible depth of flavour

Tinned peppers are great blended up to add to a tomato sauce or soup

Dairy-free cheese will provide familiarity and texture

Firm tofu gives bite and texture, as well as all-important protein

Nori helps you get a fishy, salty flavour and can be used to wrap sushi rolls

Capers offer a really individual, salty flavour

Soy cream introduces lovely silky, creamy textures

Dairy-free ice cream should always be in the freezer because, well, movie night

Fantastic feasts

Here are some delicious feasts you can create using the recipes in this book. Create your own takeaways at home, or create a spread to wow a whole dinner party, using just this book.

SPANISH SPREAD

Fancy a fiesta? Make the ultimate Spanish spread. Just add Sangria, salsa and a little bit of sunshine.
Pettigrew's Paella (page 114)
Spanish Tapas (page 187)
Proper Spanish Aioli (page 192)

THE BIG INDIAN TAKEAWAY

If contrasting curries is your thing then we've got you covered! This wonderful spread of curries, naan and rice represents the best of our favourite cuisine.
Big Bhaji Burger (page 67)
Creamy Korma (page 71)
Rogan BOSH! (page 74)
Saag Aloo Curry (page 82)
Fluffy Naan Bread & Raita (page 203)
Onion Fried Rice (page 208)

THE BIG THAI TAKEAWAY

To magic up your own Southeast Asian takeaway look no further than these recipes. You'll find deep, subtle yet strong spices and explosions of flavour.
Pad Thai (page 42)
Tom Yum Soup (page 63)
Thai Red Curry (page 78)
Massaman Curry (page 93)
(Rich Satay) Bangin' Veggie Kebabs (page 178)
Perfectly Boiled Rice (page 207)

THE BIG CHINESE TAKEAWAY

Create an Indo-Chinese takeaway in your own home. Let your guests wrap their own pancakes, and pick and choose from all the bowls in the middle of the table. Just add chopsticks.

THE BIG BBQ

Feeling like an all-year-round taste of summer? These dishes will delight any BBQ party or brighten up any dining room. Griddle and nibble to your heart's content.

ITALIAN HEAVEN

If you like pasta and pizza as much as we do, then look no further. This is the perfect dinner-party spread.

WEEKEND LUNCH

A British dinner of comfort and joy!

A TEX-MEX-STYLE FIESTA

Combine these dishes for a serious taste of Tex-Mex goodness. We hope you like guacamole (who doesn't?). Feel free to dial down the chilli if you prefer!

THE MEZZE PLATTER

Take a trip to the Middle East with the ultimate mezze spread. The flavours of hummus, falafel and olives are deliciousness in every mouthful. If you have the time, trust us, the Mezze Cake is worth it.

THE BIG BOSH! ROAST

No Sunday (or Christmas Day!) is complete without a roast dinner and all the trimmings. There are step-by-step instructions on page 127.

01

QUICK EATS

Get it done quickly
Delicious food whenever
You need a fast feed

CREAMY CARBONARA

This is everything a carbonara should be: creamy, rich and comforting. The smoky, flavourful mushrooms complement the thick, satisfying pasta sauce perfectly. A truly fantastic option for a delicious midweek dinner.

SERVES 4

6 portobello mushrooms (about 250g)
5 tbsp soy sauce
20ml maple syrup
20ml apple cider vinegar
20ml olive oil
130g cashew nuts
5 garlic cloves
190ml plant-based milk
10g nutritional yeast
150g silken tofu
300g spaghetti
125g garden peas
handful flat-leaf parsley
    or rocket leaves, to serve

Preheat oven to 200°C | Line a baking tray | Liquidiser | Small saucepan of boiling water on a high heat | Large saucepan of salted water on a high heat

Slice the mushrooms thinly | Pour the soy sauce, maple syrup, cider vinegar and olive oil into a bowl and whisk to combine | Add the mushrooms, making sure the slices are well covered in the marinade and set aside

Meanwhile, put the cashews in the small saucepan filled with boiling water and boil for 15 minutes

Take the mushroom slices out of the bowl and lay them out evenly on the lined baking tray | Add the whole garlic cloves and pour over the marinade | Bake in the hot oven for 25–30 minutes, until they have shrunk in size and begun to crisp very slightly

Drain the cashews and put them into the liquidiser along with the plant-based milk, nutritional yeast and tofu | Whizz to a very smooth cream and then set aside

Add the pasta to the large pan of boiling salted water and cook until al dente, following the instructions on the packet | Add the peas for the last minute of cooking | Fill a mug with pasta water and set aside | Drain the pasta and peas through a colander and tip the pasta back into the cooking pot

Pour the carbonara cream and 3 tablespoons of the pasta water over the pasta and stir everything around until the pasta is well covered in the cream | Take the mushrooms out of the oven and fold them into the creamy pasta | Add another splash of pasta water, if needed, to give a nice, loose, creamy consistency

Garnish with the fresh parsley or rocket (or any other green, leafy salad) and serve immediately

MUSHROOM PHO

Nothing beats a hearty pho soup. Traditionally, pho is made with a deep stock that's been brewing for hours, or even days. We've used a shortcut but retained the pho richness through the delights of shiitake mushrooms, star anise and tamarind paste. Just make sure you have enough liquid and add more water if you need to.

SERVES 6

2 onions
4 garlic cloves
15cm piece fresh ginger
3 fresh red chillies
16 shiitake mushrooms
6 tbsp sesame oil
150ml fresh orange juice
    (not from concentrate)
2 tbsp tamarind paste
4 star anise
2 cinnamon sticks
3 litres water
100ml soy or tamari sauce
100ml maple syrup
10 button mushrooms
300g flat rice noodles
4 spring onions
2 handfuls fresh coriander
2 handfuls fresh mint
150g beansprouts
200g pak choi
sriracha and soy sauce, to serve

Large saucepan on a medium heat

Peel and coarsely chop the onions and garlic | Peel the ginger by scraping off the skin with a spoon and chop coarsely | Rip the stem from one of the chillies and chop, removing the seeds if you prefer a milder flavour | Trim and roughly slice 6 of the shiitake mushrooms

Heat 3 tablespoons of the sesame oil in the large saucepan and add the chopped onion, garlic, chilli, ginger and the sliced mushrooms | Cook for 10–15 minutes, stirring continuously until everything has softened

Add the orange juice, tamarind paste, star anise and cinnamon sticks and continue to stir for another 3 minutes | Add the water, soy or tamari sauce and maple syrup

Turn up the heat, bring to the boil, then turn it down again and simmer for 10 minutes, until reduced by about one-sixth | Strain the liquid into a large bowl through a sieve | Rinse the pan

Put the pan back on a high heat and add the remaining 3 tablespoons sesame oil | While the oil is warming, trim the remaining 10 shiitake and the button mushrooms and add them to the pan | Fry for a couple of minutes, until very slightly browned | Pour all the pho liquid back into the pan | Add the rice noodles and cook for about 3–4 minutes, or according to the timings on the packet

Finely slice the spring onions and put them in a small pile on a large plate | Pick the leaves from the coriander and mint and put them on the plate | Trim and finely slice the remaining chillies, removing the seeds if you prefer a milder flavour, and put them on the plate along with the beansprouts

Trim and quarter the pak choi and add it to the soup | Take the whole pan to the table along with the plate, with a ladle for people to serve themselves and chopsticks for them to add their own fresh herbs, vegetables and chillies | Serve with soy sauce and sriracha on the side | Best eaten as soon as it's ready!

GUACARONI

Macaroni meets guacamole! This dish is as perfect as its name suggests and we think it's one of the finest pasta salads you will ever taste. It's great eaten hot or cold, served alongside a BBQ, as a lunchtime salad or with a bit of green salad as a quick main course.

SERVES 4–6

320g macaroni
3½ tsp salt
4 ripe avocados
2 limes
2 tbsp olive oil
½ tsp garlic powder
½ red onion
2 fresh red chillies
12 cherry tomatoes
20g fresh coriander leaves

Large saucepan of water on a high heat | Large mixing bowl

Add the macaroni and 2 teaspoons of the salt to the boiling water and cook until al dente, following the instructions on the packet

Halve and carefully stone the avocados by tapping the stones firmly with the heel of a knife so that it lodges in the pit, then twist and remove the stones, then scoop the flesh into the mixing bowl | Halve the limes and squeeze the juice into the bowl, catching any pips in your other hand | Add the olive oil, garlic powder and the remaining salt to taste and mash the avocado using the back of a fork | Peel and mince the onion | Rip the stems from the chillies, cut them in half lengthways and remove the seeds if you prefer a milder flavour | Finely chop the tomatoes, chillies and coriander and add to the bowl | Mix all the ingredients together

Drain the macaroni and tip into the bowl of guacamole, stirring to make sure the pasta is well covered | Serve immediately as a side dish or light lunch, or box it up ready for tomorrow's lunch

CURRY-CRUSTED SWEET POTATOES

We've mixed up the traditional stuffed potato by putting our filling on the outside in this recipe. The flavours work a treat with a fresh lime crust contrasting really well with a delicious sweet potato. This is one to freestyle with and try different flavour combos. It works great in the oven or cooked on a BBQ.

SERVES 2

2 large sweet potatoes
   (about 300g each)
vegetable oil, for greasing
salad leaves, to serve, optional
1 x portion Guacamole (shop-bought
   or see page 194), to serve, optional

FOR THE CURRY PASTE
5cm piece fresh ginger
3 garlic cloves
1 fresh red chilli
1 lime
8 sun-dried tomatoes,
   plus 1 tbsp oil from the jar
30g fresh coriander (leaves and stalks)
40g desiccated coconut
10g panko breadcrumbs
1½ tsp salt
1 tsp garam masala
1 tsp ground cumin
2 tsp water

Preheat oven to 200°C | Food processor | Baking tray | Foil

Prick the whole sweet potatoes with a fork and put them on a plate | Microwave on high for about 10–15 minutes until quite soft (alternatively put the potatoes in a 220°C oven and bake for 25 minutes, remove them from the oven and reduce the heat to 200°C) | Remove and set aside to cool down slightly | Score the skins with a sharp knife

Peel the ginger by scraping off the skin with a spoon | Peel the garlic | Rip the stem from the chilli, cut it in half lengthways and remove the seeds if you prefer a milder flavour | Cut the lime in half and squeeze the juice into the food processor, catching any pips in your other hand | Put all the rest of the curry paste ingredients into the food processor and whizz to a thick paste

Cut 2 squares of foil big enough to fully wrap your sweet potatoes in and grease one side with oil | Take half the curry paste and use your hands to encase one of the potatoes with a thick layer of paste | Repeat with the second potato

Tightly wrap the sweet potatoes in the foil squares, put on the baking tray and bake in the preheated oven for 30 minutes | Take the sweet potatoes out of the oven, remove the foil and serve with a small side salad and a big spoonful of guacamole, if using

STICKY SHIITAKE MUSHROOMS

If you're a fan of sticky, sweet, pan-Asian cuisine you will love this dish (seriously, it's bangin'!). It's quick and easy to put together and guaranteed to impress. Serve with freshly cooked rice and chopsticks.

SERVES 2

240g shiitake mushrooms
3 tbsp cornflour
2 tbsp groundnut oil
2 garlic cloves
3cm piece fresh ginger
½ tsp water
1 tbsp sesame oil
2 tbsp light brown sugar
4 tbsp dark soy sauce
2 tbsp rice wine vinegar
1 tsp sriracha sauce, or to taste
1 spring onion, to serve
250g pre-cooked basmati rice
    (shop-bought or Perfectly Boiled
    Rice, see page 207), to serve
1 tsp sesame seeds, to serve

Wok or large frying pan on a high heat

Thickly slice the mushrooms and put them in a bowl | Sprinkle 2 tablespoons of the cornflour over the top and toss everything together with your hands, making sure the mushrooms are well covered | Pour the groundnut oil into the wok or pan and get it nice and hot | Tip in the mushrooms and fry for 4–6 minutes, until cooked through and slightly crisp on the outside | Transfer the mushrooms to a bowl and set aside

Peel and finely chop the garlic and ginger | Spoon the remaining 1 tablespoon cornflour into a small dish and mix it together with the water | Wipe out the wok with kitchen paper and put it back on a low heat | Pour in the sesame oil | Add the chopped garlic and ginger and cook until you release the aromas and they're bubbling in the oil, about 1 minute | Sprinkle over the sugar and stir until caramelised, about 2 minutes more | Increase the heat slightly and pour in the cornflour mix, soy sauce and rice wine vinegar, then stir for another minute until the sauce has thickened slightly | Add the sriracha and stir it into the sauce | Tip the cooked mushrooms back into the pan and stir to warm through and completely cover in the sauce, a further 1–2 minutes

Finely slice the spring onion | Serve the chewy mushrooms over hot basmati rice, garnished with the sliced spring onion and sprinkled with sesame seeds

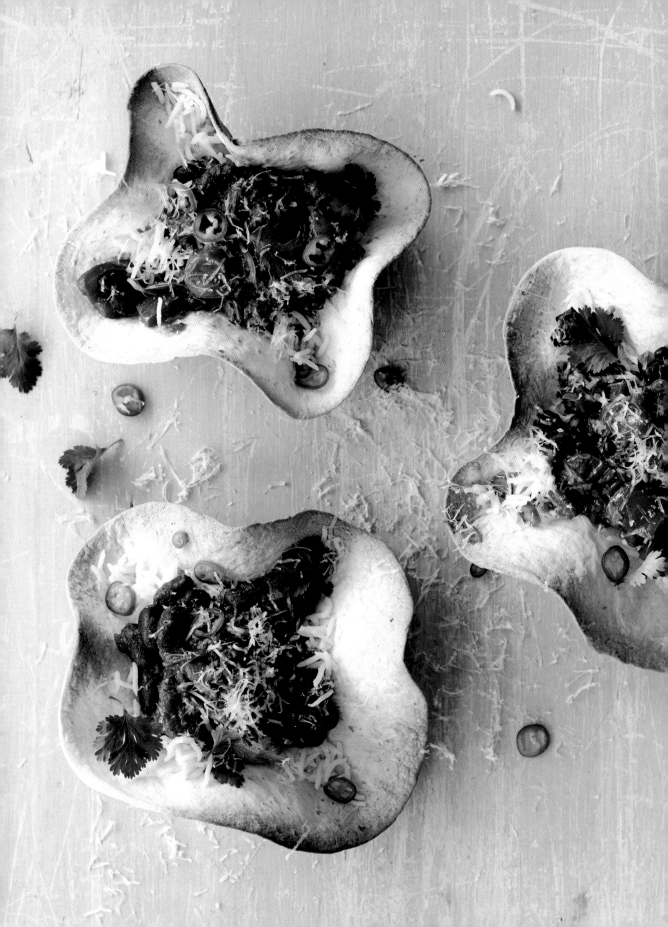

MINI CHILLI BOWLS

This is a quick-to-prepare, warming hug-in-a-bowl kind of dish that's good for impressing your guests when time is against you! Feel free to up the chilli if you like a bit of a kick. This banging chilli is served inside a cool cone dish.

SERVES 3–6

3–6 medium flour tortillas
1 fresh red chilli
1 red onion
2 garlic cloves
2 red peppers
20g fresh coriander
12 cherry tomatoes
2 tbsp olive oil
1 tsp paprika
½ tsp ground cumin
1 x 400g tin kidney beans
1 x 400g tin black beans
700g passata
500g pre-cooked rice (shop-bought or Perfectly Boiled Rice, see page 207)
50g dairy-free cheese, optional
1 lime

Preheat oven to 180°C | Muffin or cupcake tray | Lidded casserole or saucepan on a medium heat

Turn the muffin or cupcake tray upside down and place 3 tortillas in the gaps between the cups, making 3 bowl shapes | Press each tortilla down firmly to get a flat bottom, to ensure the bowls will stand up | Place the tray in the oven and bake for 7–10 minutes until lightly browned and firm | Take out of the oven and leave to cool and harden on the tray | If you are cooking for more than 3 people, repeat this step with more tortillas

Rip the stem from the chilli, cut it in half lengthways and remove the seeds if you prefer a milder flavour, then chop | Peel and chop the onion and garlic | Cut the peppers in half and cut out the stems and seeds, then chop | Cut the stalks from the coriander and finely chop, reserving the leaves for later | Halve the cherry tomatoes

Heat the olive oil in the pan and add the chopped chilli, onion, garlic and coriander stalks and cook for 5 minutes, stirring occasionally | Add the cherry tomatoes and peppers and stir for another 4–5 minutes | Add the paprika and ground cumin | Drain the kidney beans and black beans and stir into the sauce | Pour in the passata | Leave the sauce to simmer for 10 minutes, stirring occasionally

Heat the rice, following the instructions on the packet | Put a small layer of rice on the bottom of each of the tortilla bowls and top with a generous serving of chilli | Grate the dairy-free cheese, if using, on top and sprinkle over the coriander leaves | Cut the lime into wedges and place one on each plate to serve

QUICK PUTTANESCA SPAGHETTI

The combination of lemon and fresh parsley in this dish creates a voluptuous pasta and the saltiness of the capers in brine will remind you of the sea. This flexible favourite of ours is great for when you're low on fresh ingredients. It can be served with a side salad or makes a great quick meal all on its own.

SERVES 6

2 small red chillies, fresh or dried
20g flat-leaf parsley
10 Kalamata olives
4 garlic cloves
4 tbsp olive oil
1 tbsp capers, plus 1 tbsp
   of brine from the jar
½ tsp salt, plus a little extra
700g passata
500g spaghetti
220g Tenderstem broccoli
1 lemon

Large saucepan on a medium-high heat | Large saucepan of boiling salted water on a high heat

Rip the stems from the chillies, cut them in half lengthways and remove the seeds if you prefer a milder sauce, and finely chop | Separate the parsley stalks and finely chop, reserving the leaves for later | Stone and roughly chop the olives

Peel 2 of the garlic cloves | Pour 2 tablespoons of the oil into the empty saucepan, crush in the garlic and add the chillies, parsley stalks, olives and capers and stir for 2–3 minutes | Add the ½ teaspoon salt and 1 tablespoon of the salty brine water from the jar of capers | Leave to cook for a minute, then add the passata | Taste and season with salt if necessary | Turn the heat to medium and leave to simmer while you move on to the next step

Add the spaghetti to the pan of boiling water along with the remaining 2 garlic cloves | Cook until al dente, following the instructions on the packet

Meanwhile, carefully slice the broccoli stems from top to bottom, creating thin strips | Add these to the spaghetti pan for the last 30 seconds of cooking time to quickly soften | Drain the pasta and broccoli in a colander and return them to the pan | Pour over the sauce

Roughly chop the parsley leaves and add them to the pan | Pour over the remaining 2 tablespoons of oil and squeeze over the juice of a whole lemon, catching any pips in your other hand | Mix everything together and serve immediately

MINI PIZZA TARTS

These tarts are incredibly easy to prepare, really flavoursome and look impressive. They're perfect for a starter or light lunch and are an opportunity for you to get creative with your decoration. The fluffy melt-in-your-mouth crunch of the pastry makes for a decadent but messy meal!

SERVES 6

1 x 320g sheet ready-rolled dairy-free
    puff pastry
½ red onion
½ courgette
12 cherry tomatoes
6 sun-dried tomatoes
2 tbsp capers
12 pitted Kalamata olives
2 tbsp plant-based milk
50g dairy-free cheese, optional
handful small fresh basil leaves, to serve

FOR THE TOMATO SAUCE
3 tbsp tomato purée
1 tbsp olive oil
1 tbsp water
2 tsp balsamic vinegar
½ tsp pepper
½ tsp salt

Preheat oven to 180°C | Baking tray | Pastry brush

Take the puff pastry out of the packet and unroll it on to the baking tray, keeping it on the parchment paper it's wrapped in | Take a sharp knife and cut the pastry into 6 equal squares and separate them slightly | Run the tip of the knife lightly around the edge of each square to score a 1½cm border

Put all the ingredients for the tomato sauce into a small bowl and mix with a fork | Spread the sauce inside each pastry square, up to the border

Peel the red onion and trim the courgette and cherry tomatoes | Finely slice them along with the sun-dried tomatoes, capers and olives (it's important they're cut very fine so they cook quickly) | Arrange artfully over each pizza square, keeping the borders free | Brush the edges of the pizzas with the plant-based milk

Put the tray in the oven and cook for 20–22 minutes, then remove and neatly grate the dairy-free cheese, if using, over the top of each square | Put the tarts back in the oven for 3 minutes to melt (if you cook them for any longer the cheese will start to harden)

Remove the tray from the oven, scatter the basil leaves over the tartlets and serve immediately

NICE SPICE RICE

This quick and easy dish is a regular late-night meal in the BOSH! studio. It's healthy, colourful and also delicious, with a salty, sweet, nutty flavour and an incredible number of healthy veg. Works great as a quick meal or a side, or as a leftover lunch the following day!

SERVES 3–4

100g kale
20g fresh coriander
2 large garlic cloves
5cm piece fresh ginger
1 large fresh red chilli
5 spring onions
1 red pepper
1 tbsp coconut oil
1 tbsp toasted sesame oil
25ml maple syrup
4 tbsp light soy sauce
80g baby corn
60g small asparagus shoots
80g sugar snap peas
80g sprouting broccoli
120g smooth peanut butter
30ml water
500g cooked basmati rice
    (shop-bought or pre-cooked)
sriracha sauce, to serve, optional
fresh lime, to serve, optional
salt

Wok on a medium heat

Chop the kale and coriander and set aside | Peel and finely slice the garlic | Peel the ginger by scraping off the skin with a spoon and finely slice | Rip the stem from the chilli then cut it in half lengthways and remove the seeds if you prefer a milder flavour | Finely chop the chilli and spring onions | Cut the pepper in half and cut out the stem and seeds, then cut into bite-sized chunks along with the rest of the vegetables | Measure out the oils, syrup and soy sauce into saucers or small bowls ready to use

Add the coconut oil to the wok and stir until melted | Add the toasted sesame oil and let it infuse into the coconut oil | Add the garlic and ginger and stir them around for 1–2 minutes, until the ginger looks like it's begun to froth

Add the chopped chilli and spring onions and stir until the onions have softened | Pour in the maple syrup and soy sauce and stir | Add the corn, asparagus and red pepper and stir for roughly 1 minute | Throw in the sugar snap peas and broccoli and stir for another minute | Add the peanut butter and water to the pan and stir until all the vegetables are well covered | Finally, add the kale and stir until it is slightly wilted | Taste and season with salt if necessary | Turn the heat down to low

Add the rice to the wok and fold it into the vegetables for 2 minutes | Sprinkle over the coriander and briefly stir through | Serve immediately with wedges of fresh lime and sriracha sauce on the side, if using

EASY PEASY PASTA

The clue is in the name with this one. It's an effortlessly simple pasta sauce that can be made with minimal effort, since it's mainly just roasted vegetables. It's a regular supper at BOSH! HQ. It's fresh, filling and gives you loads of your daily vegetables in one lavish meal. Try serving it up with a side salad and some crusty bread.

SERVES 4

2 red onions
4 garlic cloves
2 red peppers
100g sun-dried tomatoes
40g baby leaf spinach
50g capers
2 small courgettes
100g pitted Kalamata olives
500g cherry tomatoes
8 tbsp oil (ideally from the
    sun-dried tomato jar!)
350g passata
320g fusilli
30g basil leaves
salt and black pepper

Preheat oven to 180°C | 20 x 30cm lasagne dish | Large saucepan

Peel and finely slice the onions and garlic | Cut the peppers in half, cut out the stems and seeds and slice into thin strips | Slice the sun-dried tomatoes | Finely chop the spinach leaves and capers and chop the courgettes into bite-sized chunks | Halve the olives and tomatoes | Put all the vegetables into the lasagne dish and season all over with salt and pepper | Pour over the oil and passata and stir to ensure all the vegetables are covered | Cover the dish with foil and put it in the oven to roast for 30 minutes

Take the dish out of the oven, remove the foil, stir everything and put the dish back in the oven for a further 15 minutes

Meanwhile, boil the kettle and pour the boiling water into a large pan on a high heat | Add the pasta and a big pinch of salt and cook until al dente, following the instructions on the packet | Drain the cooked pasta through a colander and tip it back into the pan

Take the lasagne dish out of the oven, stir in the basil leaves and pour your freshly roasted veggie sauce over the pasta | Stir so that it's well mixed, serve and enjoy!

PAD THAI

In Thailand, pad Thai was a regular lunch for us (and the perfect remedy for a Thai-bucket-induced hangover). It varies everywhere you go, but typically includes the artful placement of fresh lime, peanuts and spring onions around the bowl. We like to replicate this and serve it with chilli flakes, sweet chilli sauce and sriracha.

SERVES 4

140g extra-firm tofu
1 tbsp cornflour
4 tbsp vegetable oil
200g flat dried rice noodles
½ onion
2 garlic cloves
1 fresh red chilli
1 carrot
splash of water
100g beansprouts
3 limes
4 tbsp soy sauce
2 spring onions
8 tbsp unsalted peanuts
1 tbsp chilli flakes, to serve
sweet chilli sauce, to serve, optional
sriracha sauce, to serve, optional

FOR THE DRESSING
1 tbsp palm sugar (or any sugar)
2 tbsp tamarind paste
1 tbsp chilli sauce

Tofu press or 2 clean tea towels and a weight such as a heavy book | Wok

Press the tofu using a tofu press or place it between two clean tea towels, lay it on a plate and put a weight on top | Leave for at least half an hour to drain any liquid and firm up before you start cooking

In a bowl, mix together all the ingredients for the dressing

Take half the tofu and cut it into 1cm cubes (save the other half for another time) | Sift over the cornflour and turn the tofu to coat all over

Put the wok on a high heat and pour in 2 tablespoons of oil | Add the tofu and immediately reduce the heat to medium | Stir gently, without breaking up the tofu, until lightly browned | Transfer to a plate

Boil a kettle | Put the noodles in a bowl, cover them with the hot water and leave for about 3 minutes, until they're flexible but not cooked (check the packet instructions to make sure you don't fully cook them) | Drain and run under cold water | Set aside

Peel and chop the onion and garlic | Rip the stem from the chilli and chop, removing the seeds if you prefer a milder flavour | Trim the carrot and cut into matchsticks

Put the wok back on a high heat and add the remaining 2 tablespoons of oil | Add the onion, garlic and chilli and cook, stirring regularly, for 1–2 minutes | Add the carrot and cook for another 1–2 minutes | Add the noodles, dressing and a splash of water | Fry for a few minutes until the vegetables are tender

Return the tofu to the wok with the beansprouts | Cut 1 lime in half and squeeze in the juice, catching any pips in your other hand | Add the soy sauce | Stir-fry until the vegetables are slightly soft but still crunchy | Remove from the heat | Taste and add soy or chilli sauce if needed

Slice the green part of the spring onions into long, thin strips | Break up the peanuts | Cut the remaining limes into wedges

Divide the pad Thai between bowls with piles of sliced onion, peanuts, lime wedges and chilli flakes | Serve with sweet chilli sauce or sriracha on the side, if using

PORTOBELLO MUSHROOM BURGERS

The herbs are absolutely delicious in this dish and perfectly complement the earthy, rustic flavour of the portobello mushrooms. You could make these with pitta bread if you want a healthier option, then fill the bread with as many veggies as you see fit.

SERVES 4

8 portobello mushrooms (about 325g)
4 garlic cloves
6 sprigs fresh thyme
3 sprigs fresh rosemary
4 tsp olive oil
4 tsp balsamic glaze
4 good-quality burger buns
1 beef tomato
1 baby gem lettuce
½ small red onion
4 tbsp ketchup
4 tbsp vegan mayonnaise
salt and black pepper

Preheat oven to 200°C or heat the BBQ | Cut 8 squares of foil big enough to wrap your mushrooms | Baking sheet

Lay the mushrooms out on a clean surface with the stalks pointing up | Peel and mince the garlic and spread it evenly over the mushrooms | Remove the leaves from the herbs by running your thumb and forefinger from the top to the base of the stems (the leaves should easily come away), then finely chop and sprinkle evenly over the mushrooms

Drizzle each mushroom with olive oil and balsamic glaze and lightly season with salt and pepper | Wrap each mushroom in a square of foil and place them on the baking sheet or on the hot BBQ | Put the tray in the oven, if using, and cook for 20 minutes

Meanwhile, slice the burger buns in half | Slice the tomato, separate the lettuce leaves and peel and thinly slice the onion | Drizzle some ketchup over the base of each bun and vegan mayo over the tops

Take the mushrooms out of the oven or off the BBQ | Carefully remove the foil (watch out for steam) and place 2 mushrooms on each bun base | Add the tomato slices, a couple of lettuce leaves and a few slices of onion, put the tops on and enjoy

CRISPY CHILLI TOFU

This is our take on one of our favourite Chinese takeaway dishes. It's spicy, full of umami flavour, sticky, gooey and incredibly moreish. Often when you buy this kind of dish it's filled with MSG, but ours is much healthier, with a base of orange juice and sweet chilli sauce adding the main sweet tang. Serve with Perfectly Boiled Rice (see page 207) or Special Fried Rice (see page 209).

SERVES 2–4

1 x 280g block firm tofu

150g cornflour

vegetable oil, for frying

2 lemons

250ml orange juice

100g sweet chilli sauce

1 tbsp sriracha or other chilli sauce

3 tbsp soy sauce

1 spring onion, to serve

1 tsp sesame seeds, to serve

Tofu press or 2 clean tea towels and a weight such as a heavy book | Large, deep frying pan on a high heat | Large plate covered with kitchen paper

First, press the tofu using a tofu press or place it between two clean tea towels, lay it on a plate and put a weight on top | Leave for at least half an hour to drain any liquid and firm up before you start cooking

Carefully slice the pressed tofu into 1cm-wide sticks and spread them out on a board | Sift cornflour over the top, coating the pieces generously | Use tongs or two forks to turn the pieces and sift over more cornflour until the tofu is covered on all sides | The thicker the better with the cornflour as this coating gives the cooked tofu its crunchy texture

Pour enough oil into the pan to fully coat the bottom and heat until it makes the tip of a wooden spoon sizzle | Carefully place the tofu pieces in the pan, with a bit of space around each one (you may need to cook them in batches) | Cook for 5 minutes, turning the pieces every minute or so until they are starting to turn golden brown | Transfer to the plate lined with kitchen paper | Tip away the excess oil in the pan and reduce the heat to medium-high

Cut the lemons in half and squeeze the juice into the pan, catching any pips in your other hand (be careful as the pan may spit) | Add the orange juice, sweet chilli sauce, sriracha and soy sauce and bring to the boil | Simmer for 5–7 minutes until the liquid has reduced to a syrupy consistency

Add the tofu strips back to the pan and stir until fully coated | Continue to cook, stirring regularly, for 5 minutes and then remove from the heat | Finely slice the spring onion and sprinkle over the tofu along with the sesame seeds before serving

JACKFRUIT TACOS

Jackfruit is a fantastic and crowd-pleasing ingredient with a fibrous texture and flesh that soaks up flavour brilliantly, but it can be hard to find. Try your local Asian supermarket and be sure to choose green jackfruit in water. These tacos are perfect finger food, combining tasty jackfruit with a Mexican combo of zingy salsa and creamy guacamole.

SERVES 6

1 x serving Guacamole
    (shop-bought or see page 194)
1 x serving Salsa (shop-bought
    or see page 195)
1 x 400g tin young green jackfruit
    in water
1 white onion
4 garlic cloves
1 tbsp vegetable oil
1 tbsp maple syrup
100ml vegetable stock
½ tsp Tabasco sauce
4 limes
1½ tsp ground cumin
1½ tsp smoked paprika
½–1 tsp chilli powder
½ tsp salt
handful fresh coriander
12 crunchy taco shells

Deep frying pan with a lid on a medium heat

If you're making your own guacamole and salsa, do this first following the instructions on pages 194 and 195

Tip the jackfruit into a sieve or colander to drain off the excess water and pat the pieces down with a clean tea towel to dry them off | Cut into 5mm strips and put to one side

Peel and slice the onion and garlic very thinly | Warm the vegetable oil in the frying pan | Add the onion and garlic to the pan and stir with a wooden spoon until soft and translucent | Add the jackfruit, maple syrup, vegetable stock and Tabasco sauce | Cut 1 of the limes in half and squeeze in the juice of one half, catching any pips in your other hand | Stir until the jackfruit is well covered

Put the lid on the pan, turn down the heat and let it simmer for 7–10 minutes, stirring occasionally, until the liquid has been absorbed into the jackfruit | Take the lid off the pan and sprinkle over all the spices and the salt | Stir until the jackfruit pieces are well covered and taking on the colour of the spices | Transfer the jackfruit pieces to a serving dish

Slice the remaining limes into wedges and remove the leaves from the coriander by running your thumb and forefinger from the top to the base of the stems (the leaves should easily come away), saving the stalks for another recipe | Serve the taco shells, jackfruit, guacamole, salsa, lime wedges and coriander leaves on individual plates and let everyone build their own tacos

SWEET & SOUR CRISPY TOFU

Sweet and sour needs no introduction! This dish is an indulgent worldwide classic made with smooth, soft tofu. It's made even more delicious by the addition of pineapple, and the way the crispy fried tofu contrasts with the sweet syrupy sauce. Mix this with any other Asian dish and boiled rice and you have a winner on your hands.

SERVES 2–4

1 x 280g block of firm tofu
6cm piece fresh ginger
1 red onion
1 garlic clove
1 green pepper
200ml pineapple juice
60ml rice vinegar
60ml tomato ketchup
70g light brown sugar
1 tsp garlic powder
1 tsp onion powder, optional
4 tbsp cornflour
2 tbsp vegetable oil
2 tbsp sesame oil
½ tsp chilli flakes
½ tsp salt
100g tinned pineapple chunks

Small saucepan on a low-medium heat | Tofu press or 2 clean tea towels and a weight such as a heavy book | 2 x large frying pans on a medium-high heat | Fine grater

Press the tofu using a tofu press, or place it between two clean tea towels, lay it on a plate and put a weight on top | Leave for at least half an hour to drain any liquid and firm up before you start cooking

Peel the ginger by scraping off the skin with a spoon and then grate it | Peel and finely slice the red onion and the garlic | Cut the pepper in half and cut out the stem and seeds | Chop the pepper into 2cm chunks

Put the pineapple juice, rice vinegar, ketchup and sugar in the small saucepan and stir to dissolve the sugar | Increase the heat to medium-high and let it bubble away for about 7 minutes until you have a syrupy sauce | Take the saucepan off the heat and set aside

Put the garlic powder and the onion powder, if using, into a large bowl with the cornflour and mix together | Carefully cut the drained tofu into 1cm chunks and add them to the bowl | Toss them gently in the cornflour mix until they're well covered

Heat the vegetable oil in one of the large frying pans | Add the tofu chunks and fry until they have started to brown and formed a crispy coating, about 7–10 minutes (be delicate as you stir the cubes, you want to keep them intact) | Take the pan off the heat and set aside

Meanwhile, heat the sesame oil in the second frying pan | Add the onion slices and stir until translucent, about 5 minutes | Add the green pepper, chilli flakes, salt, garlic and ginger and continue to cook for another 3–5 minutes, stirring all the time | Drain the pineapple and add to the pan, continuing to stir until the pineapple is warm | Tip the tofu into the pan and heat | Pour over the sweet and sour sauce and fold it around the vegetables so that everything is well covered and warmed through, another 1–2 minutes

IRRESISTIBLE RISOTTO

This risotto is bursting with colour, flavour and healthy goodness. We're big fans of getting as much green into our bodies as possible to give us the vital nutrients we need. This dish is testament to that, but it's also delicious. Cook slowly, add the stock bit by bit and you'll have a dish guaranteed to please!

SERVES 4

60g macadamia nuts

1 medium red onion

2 large garlic cloves

3 tbsp mixed fresh herbs, such as sage, parsley and mint

75g green beans

60g asparagus

60g kale

½ lemon

900ml vegetable stock

2 tbsp olive oil

225g risotto rice, such as Arborio or Carnaroli

125ml dry white wine

75g garden peas

3 tbsp nutritional yeast

1½ tbsp dairy-free butter

salt and black pepper

Preheat oven to 160°C | Small baking tray | Medium saucepan on a low heat | Medium saucepan on a medium heat

Spread the macadamia nuts over the small baking tray, put the tray in the oven and toast for 5–8 minutes, until golden | Leave to cool slightly, then roughly chop

Meanwhile, peel and finely chop the red onion and garlic | Chop the herbs | Slice the green beans into 2cm pieces | Snap the tough ends off the asparagus and cut the stems into 1cm pieces | Remove the tough stems from the kale and roughly chop | Finely grate the zest of the lemon

Pour the stock into the medium saucepan on a low heat and keep warm

Add the olive oil to the other pan | Add the chopped onions and cook until they begin to soften, about 10–15 minutes | Add the garlic and stir for another minute | Pour in the rice and toast for a further minute

Turn up the heat slightly and pour in the white wine | Simmer until the liquid has almost completely evaporated, stirring frequently | Add the green beans and asparagus to the pan and give everything a stir

Now start adding a ladleful of stock at a time, stirring continuously and waiting for the stock to be absorbed before adding the next ladleful | After 8 minutes, add the peas and kale to the pan and continue to cook for a further 6–8 minutes, until the rice is just cooked and the vegetables are tender (you might have a little stock left over)

Remove the pan from the heat, stir in the chopped herbs, nutritional yeast, lemon zest, macadamia nuts and dairy-free butter | Season to taste with salt and pepper and serve immediately

TOM YUM SOUP

This was Henry's dish of choice as he travelled around Thailand. The healthy, spicy Thai classic just feels like holiday. As a soup it's surprisingly filling, and it's best eaten when it's so hot and spicy it's hard to continue and you break into sweats! Slurping is good here. Let this gorgeously hot, spicy soup warm you to your core!

SERVES 4

4 tbsp olive oil
1 small onion
4 garlic cloves
2 fresh red chillies
2½cm piece fresh ginger
1½ litres vegetable stock
1 tsp tomato purée
2 lemongrass stalks
6 lime leaves
2 limes
1 x 250g pack chestnut mushrooms
100g enoki mushrooms (2 bunches)
200g cherry tomatoes
1 x 225g tin water chestnuts, optional
4 spring onions, to serve
small handful fresh chives, to serve
small handful fresh coriander, to serve

FOR THE TOM YUM PASTE
2 tbsp vegetable oil
100g Thai Red Curry Paste (see page 78)
3 tbsp palm sugar
1 tsp salt

Wok on a medium heat | Kettle boiled

First make the tom yum paste | Add the vegetable oil to the wok | When it's hot add the red curry paste, palm sugar and salt and fry for 3 minutes, until the paste goes a darker red colour | Remove from the heat and scrape into a bowl | Give the wok a quick rinse and put back on the heat

Add the olive oil to the clean wok | Peel and roughly chop the onion | Peel the garlic | Rip the stems from the chillies and finely slice one, removing the seeds if you prefer a milder flavour | Peel the ginger by scraping off the skin with a spoon and finely chop | Crush the garlic into the wok, add in the onion, chilli and ginger and cook for 4 minutes to allow the flavours to infuse

Pour 500ml of the stock into the wok and bring to the boil | Add the tom yum paste and mix well | Add the remaining stock and the tomato purée | Bash the bases of the lemongrass stalks and add them to the pan | Slice the lime leaves and throw them in | Simmer for 20 minutes

Cut the limes in half and squeeze in the juice, catching any pips in your other hand | Halve the chestnut mushrooms and add them to the pan with the enoki mushrooms and the tomatoes | Slice the water chestnuts, if using, and add them to the pan | Finely slice the remaining chilli into long diagonal slices, removing the seeds if you prefer a milder flavour, and add to the pan | Simmer for a further 5 minutes

Divide the soup between bowls | Trim and slice the spring onions and chop the chives | Sprinkle over the soup along with the coriander leaves and serve

PASTA CAPONATA

This hearty dish features a rich Sicilian caponata sauce, complete with pine nuts and raisins, which has great depth of flavour, but with an added celery crunch and kick of chilli. Feel free to use more or less garlic (we like lots of garlic!) and then serve with bread to soak up all the juices.

SERVES 4–6

2 aubergines (about 500g)
300g cherry tomatoes
3 tbsp olive oil
1½ tsp chilli flakes
1 red onion
3 garlic cloves
1 celery stick
2 tbsp tomato purée
1 x 400g tin chopped tomatoes
1 tsp dried oregano
2 sprigs fresh thyme
30g small capers
40g raisins
60g pitted Kalamata olives
500g penne pasta
10g dark chocolate
20g fresh parsley
1 tbsp balsamic vinegar
40g pine nuts
salt and black pepper

Preheat oven to 180°C | Line a baking tray | Large frying pan with lid on a medium heat | Large saucepan | Small frying pan

Trim the aubergines and chop the flesh into 2cm cubes | Lay on the lined baking tray along with the cherry tomatoes and drizzle over 1 tablespoon of the olive oil | Sprinkle with a good layer of salt, pepper and the chilli flakes, put the tray in the preheated oven and bake for 30 minutes

Meanwhile, pour the remaining 2 tablespoons of oil into the large frying pan | Peel and finely chop the onion and garlic and add to the pan | Trim the leaves and root from the celery, then finely chop and add to the pan | Cook the onions, garlic and celery for 10–15 minutes, stirring regularly, until they are soft and translucent

Add the tomato purée to the pan and stir | Add the chopped tomatoes, oregano, thyme, capers, raisins and olives, plus a little salt and pepper to taste, then reduce the heat to a gentle simmer and let everything cook for 5 minutes | Remove the roasted aubergines and tomatoes from the oven and add them to the pan, giving everything a stir | Put the lid on and simmer for 12–15 minutes, stirring every 5 minutes to stop it burning

Boil a kettle and fill the large saucepan with the boiling water and a pinch of salt | Add the pasta and cook until al dente, following the instructions on the packet | Strain away the water and tip the cooked pasta back into the pasta pan

Meanwhile, chop or grate the dark chocolate and sprinkle it into the caponata sauce | Chop the stalks from the parsley and save for another recipe, then chop the leaves and add three-quarters to the pan along with the balsamic vinegar | Simmer for a further 3–5 minutes with the lid off | Taste and season if necessary | Pour the sauce over the pasta and fold it in, making sure everything is well covered

Put the small frying pan on a medium-high heat and toast the pine nuts in the dry pan until golden | Sprinkle over the pasta along with the reserved parsley leaves before serving

BIG BHAJI BURGER

This juxtaposition of Indian cuisine with the classic American burger works incredibly well. It's a fantastic fusion of flavours that are really big and satisfying, and you can play with really interesting toppings. These are great with Jane's Mint Raita (see page 204), or make smaller bhaji bites and serve them with curry.

MAKES 6

500ml–1 litre vegetable oil, for deep frying
2 red onions
6cm piece fresh ginger
1 fresh red chilli
20g fresh coriander leaves
1½ tsp coriander seeds
1½ tsp cumin seeds
300g gram flour
1½ tsp garam masala
200ml water
4 good-quality burger buns
3 tbsp vegan mayonnaise, to serve
¼ small cucumber, to serve
1 large tomato, to serve
1 avocado, to serve
1 baby gem lettuce, to serve
2 tbsp mango chutney, to serve
1 poppadum, to serve
salt

Large saucepan on a high heat | Cooking thermometer, optional | Pestle and mortar | Line a dinner plate with kitchen paper

Pour the vegetable oil into the large saucepan so that it comes no more than two-thirds up the side of the pan | Heat the oil to 180°C, or until a wooden spoon dipped into the oil sizzles around the edges

Meanwhile, peel and very finely slice the onions and put them into a big bowl | Peel the ginger by scraping off the skin with a spoon and finely chop | Rip the stem from the chilli, cut it in half lengthways and remove the seeds if you prefer a milder flavour, then finely chop and add to the pan | Roughly chop the coriander leaves | Add the ginger, chilli and coriander to the bowl | Crush the coriander and cumin seeds with a pestle and mortar or the end of a rolling pin and add them to the bowl | Add the gram flour, garam masala, water and a generous pinch of salt and mix until everything is well combined and covered with a wet sticky batter

Divide the mixture into 6 and use your hands to mould it into patties around 9cm wide and no more than 1cm thick | Use a metal spoon to carefully lower 2 of the patties into the hot oil and cook them for about 5 minutes, flipping them over halfway | Remove the patties when they are golden and crisp and transfer to the plate lined with kitchen paper to drain any excess oil | Repeat with the remaining patties

While the bhajis are frying, slice the burger buns in half and spread the bottom halves with vegan mayonnaise | Thinly slice the cucumber and tomato | Halve and carefully stone the avocado by tapping the stone firmly with the heel of a knife so that it lodges in the pit, then twist and remove the stone | Run a dessert spoon around the inside of the avocado skin to scoop out the flesh, then slice finely

To serve the bhaji burgers, lay a few lettuce leaves on the bottom of the burger buns and place the burgers on top | Spread a little mango chutney on top of each, followed by slices of tomato, avocado and cucumber | Break up the poppadum and sprinkle it over the top before closing the buns

CREAMY SEASIDE PIE

Nothing says 'taste of the British seaside' more than a fish pie, so we've replicated that flavour with a clever combination of mushrooms, capers and lemon. Topped with crispy but fluffy potato, this hearty, healthy dish is guaranteed to impress your guests and warm your cockles. The different mushroom shapes give a wonderfully varied texture to this dish, just like a fish pie.

SERVES 6

1 large white onion
4 garlic cloves
600g mixed mushrooms (this works best with Japanese mushrooms like shiitake, oyster mushrooms, buna shimeji, shiro shimeji, eryngii or king oysters, enoki, golden enoki, maitake or a mixture)
3 tbsp olive oil
2 sheets sushi nori
100ml white wine
1 tbsp salt, plus a little extra
50ml plant-based milk
1 tbsp wholegrain mustard
2 tbsp nutritional yeast
2 tbsp capers
1 tbsp caper brine
1 lemon
175ml soy cream
200g frozen peas
30g parsley leaves
black pepper

FOR THE POTATO TOPPING
1.4kg Maris Piper or other fluffy potatoes
3 tbsp dairy-free butter, plus a little extra
125ml soy cream
50ml plant-based milk
1 tsp wholegrain mustard
1 tbsp nutritional yeast
salt and black pepper

Preheat oven to 180°C | Large, deep frying pan on a medium heat | Large saucepan with lid | 20 x 30cm lasagne dish

To make the topping, peel the potatoes and cut into large chunks | Put them in the large saucepan and add enough cold water to cover them | And a big pinch of salt | Turn on the heat to high and bring the water to the boil, then cover the pan partially with a lid and simmer for 15–20 minutes, until the potatoes are tender when pierced with a knife | Drain through a colander then tip the potatoes back into the pan and set aside

Meanwhile, peel and finely chop the onion and the garlic and roughly chop the mushrooms | Warm the oil in the large frying pan | Add the chopped onions to the pan and cook for 10 minutes, until soft (cook them slowly to make sure they don't burn and to draw out the flavour)

Use scissors to cut the nori into 1cm pieces and sprinkle them into the pan | Increase the heat to medium-high and add the chopped garlic and mushrooms | Cook for about 10 minutes, until soft, slightly golden and significantly reduced in size (the pan will be very full to start) | Pour in the white wine and cook until reduced by half, another 2–3 minutes

Reduce the heat to medium and add 1 tablespoon of salt, the plant-based milk, mustard and the nutritional yeast | Add the capers and the tablespoon of brine from the jar | Cut the lemon in half and squeeze in the juice, catching any pips with your other hand | Stir everything around and continue to cook until the mushrooms have soaked up around half the liquid, about 10 minutes | Pour the soy cream into the pan and stir everything together so that the sauce has a nice creamy texture

Add the peas to the pan, folding them in so that they're well mixed | Take the pan off the heat | Roughly chop the parsley and stir it through the mixture | Pour the mushroom filling into the lasagne dish

Return to the potatoes | Add the dairy-free butter, soy cream, plant-based milk, mustard and nutritional yeast to the potatoes and mash together until thick and creamy | Taste and season with salt and pepper

Spoon the mashed potato on top of the mushroom filling and carefully smooth it out to the edges of the dish | Use a fork to scrape lines across the top | Flake over bits of dairy-free butter, if you like, to help the potato crisp up | Put in the oven and bake for 20 minutes, then put under a hot grill for 2–3 minutes so it has a crispy crust with golden brown peaks

CREAMY KORMA

Korma is often thought of as an accessible beginner's curry. But, let's be honest, that's because it's downright delicious. We love a creamy korma. It's a dish that's close to our hearts. This one is healthy, tasty and full of hearty flavour. Trust us, you're going to love it. Feel free to use any combination of roast vegetables you like. Serve with rice (see page 207) or Naan (see page 203).

SERVES 4–6

Preheat oven to 180°C | Line a baking tray | Liquidiser | Large frying pan

1 large sweet potato (about 400g)
½ butternut squash (about 500g)
2 carrots (about 150g)
3 tbsp vegetable oil
2 large white onions
7 green cardamom pods
1½ tsp poppy seeds
2 cloves
1 bay leaf
50g cashew nuts
75g blanched almonds
2cm piece fresh ginger
2 fresh green chillies
3 garlic cloves
½ tsp ground nutmeg
½ tsp ground turmeric
1 x 400ml tin coconut milk
2 limes
small bunch of fresh coriander, to serve
2 spring onions, to serve
rice, to serve, optional
salt

Peel the sweet potato, squash and carrots | Cut into 2cm chunks and arrange on the lined baking tray | Drizzle with 1 tablespoon of the oil and season lightly with salt | Put the tray in the oven and roast for 30 minutes, turning the tray in the oven after 20 minutes if necessary | Remove when softened and a little brown | Peel and finely slice the onions

Bash the cardamom pods with the end of a knife and tear them open | Tip the seeds into the large frying pan | Add the poppy seeds and cloves and put on a medium-high heat | Toast for 2 minutes

Reduce the heat to medium-low | Add the remaining 2 tablespoons of oil | Add the onions, bay leaf, cashews and 50g of the blanched almonds | Stir and cook for 12 minutes, until the onions are soft and the nuts slightly golden, stirring regularly

Peel the ginger by scraping off the skin with a spoon, then roughly chop | Rip the stems from the chillies, cut them in half lengthways and remove the seeds if you prefer a milder sauce, then finely chop | Peel and crush the garlic into the pan | Add the ginger, chilli, ground nutmeg and turmeric to the pan | Cook for another 2 minutes

Take off the heat and cool for 5 minutes | Remove the bay leaf | Transfer to the liquidiser with 200ml coconut milk and whizz to a smooth paste, about 60 seconds | Pour back into the pan and put on a medium heat

Add the roasted vegetables to the pan | Pour in the rest of the coconut milk and stir gently until well mixed | Reduce the heat and simmer for about 5 minutes | Add a splash of water if the sauce is too thick

Cut the limes in half and squeeze the juice over the curry, catching any pips in your other hand | Season to taste with salt

Divide between 4–6 plates and serve with rice, if using | Chop the stalks from the coriander and save for another recipe, then chop the leaves and the rest of the blanched almonds and slice the spring onions | Scatter a little over each portion

PASTABALL MARINARA

This inside-out pasta dish is insanely delicious! We were coming up with revolutionary burger recipes and, like Einstein creating relativity, realised we could make meatballs out of pasta. The tomato sauce is one of the lushest, thickest pasta sauces we have ever created – it's truly scrumptious. If you prefer less sugar, substitute vegan pesto for the BBQ sauce.

SERVES 4

250g wholewheat pasta shapes, such as penne
1 x 400g tin black beans
50g sun-dried tomatoes in oil
1 tbsp chilli powder
50ml BBQ sauce
olive oil
1 large onion
2 garlic cloves
a few small fresh basil leaves, to serve
salt and black pepper

FOR THE MARINARA SAUCE
1 large onion
3 garlic cloves
olive oil
260ml red wine
1½ tbsp dried oregano
1 bay leaf
75g tomato purée
75ml water
900g tomatoes
15g fresh basil leaves
½ tsp sugar

Preheat oven to 180°C | Line a baking tray | Large deep frying pan with a lid on a medium heat | Kettle boiled | Large saucepan | Food processor | Frying pan

To make the sauce, peel and finely chop the onion and garlic | Add some oil to the large frying pan and cook the onions for 7 minutes, stirring occasionally, until softened | Add the garlic and cook for another minute, until the smell of the garlic fills the room | Add the red wine and stir, then cook for a further 5 minutes until the wine is bubbling and starting to thicken | Add the oregano and bay leaf and stir | Add the tomato purée and water and stir again

Finely chop the tomatoes and scrape them into the pan with all the juices | Tear the basil leaves into the pan and stir everything together | Add the sugar and some salt and pepper to taste | Put the lid on the pan, reduce the heat to medium-low and leave to simmer for 15–25 minutes, stirring occasionally (the longer you leave it, the richer the sauce) | Uncover and simmer for a further 10 minutes | When it's ready the sauce should be rich, luscious and thick | Taste and adjust the seasoning if necessary

While the sauce is simmering, pour the boiling water into the large saucepan and add a pinch of salt | Bring to the boil, add the pasta and cook until al dente, following the instructions on the packet | Drain and rinse the pasta under cold water for 30 seconds to cool it to room temperature

Tip the cold, cooked pasta into the food processor | Drain the black beans and the sun-dried tomatoes and add them to the food processor along with the chilli powder, sun-dried tomatoes and BBQ sauce | Blend to a thick paste, then pour the mixture into a large bowl

Place another frying pan on a medium heat and add a little oil | Peel and finely chop the remaining onion and 2 garlic cloves | Add the onion to the hot pan and cook for around 15 minutes, until soft | Add the garlic and stir it around until you've released the aroma (a minute or so) | Tip the onions and garlic into the bowl with the pasta and mix everything together | Add a little salt and pepper to taste

Wet your hands to stop the mixture sticking | Pull small pieces of the mixture out of the bowl and shape them into 3cm balls | Arrange the balls on the lined baking tray

Add a little olive oil to the pan you used to cook the onions and put it on a medium-high heat | When the pan is nice and hot, add the balls in batches, turning them over regularly until they brown all over, about 3–5 minutes | Transfer the browned pastaballs to the lined baking tray and, once all the batches are done, put the tray in the oven | Bake for 10 minutes

To serve, put a couple of large spoonfuls of the sauce into serving bowls and top each with 4 pastaballs | Garnish with a few torn-up basil leaves and a drizzle of olive oil | Serve immediately

ROGAN BOSH!

This is our take on a Kashmiri speciality curry. It's meant to be red, rustic and spicy. We've used our favourite vegetable – aubergine – and coconut yoghurt to give the creamy texture, but you could use different veggies if you prefer. Serve with Naan (see page 203), Perfectly Boiled Rice (see page 207), or on its own for a lighter dish.

SERVES 2–4

4 garlic cloves
4cm piece fresh ginger
3 fresh red chillies
1 tbsp tomato purée
60ml water
1 large aubergine
3 tbsp vegetable oil
4 green cardamom pods
1 onion
6 black peppercorns
1 bay leaf
1½cm cinnamon stick
1 tsp sugar
1 tsp ground cumin
2 tsp ground coriander
100g coconut yoghurt
large pinch of garam masala
handful fresh coriander, to serve
handful desiccated coconut flakes, to serve
salt

Liquidiser | Large frying pan on medium-high heat | Large saucepan with a lid

Peel the garlic and ginger and put them into the liquidiser | Rip the stems from 2 of the chillies, removing the seeds if you prefer a milder sauce, and add them to the liquidiser | Add the tomato purée and 60ml water and blend to a smooth paste (add more water if needed)

Trim the aubergine and cut it into 1 x 3cm chunks | Add 2 tablespoons of the oil to the large frying pan | Add the aubergine and cook for about 10–15 minutes, turning regularly, until well browned on each side

While the aubergine is cooking, put the cardamom pods in a mortar and pestle and bash them to release the seeds (or use the end of a rolling pin) | Discard the shells | Peel and finely chop the onion

When the aubergine is browned, tip it on to a plate and set aside | Add the remaining oil to the pan along with the cardamom, peppercorns, bay leaf and cinnamon and fry for 2 minutes | Add the chopped onion and sugar | Reduce the heat to medium and sauté for about 10–15 minutes, stirring the onions until they've softened (add a splash more oil to the pan if the onions begin to stick)

Add the ginger paste from the liquidiser to the saucepan | Add the ground cumin and coriander and mix everything together well | Put the pan on a medium-high heat and fry for 5 minutes, stirring regularly | Add the aubergine cubes and stir well | Add the coconut yoghurt and stir it in (if it's too thick, add a little water to loosen – you want a thick, gravy-like consistency) | Cover with the lid and cook for 5 minutes

Rip the stem from the remaining chilli, cut it in half lengthways and remove the seeds if you prefer a milder flavour, then slice finely | Taste the curry and season with salt or garam masala as necessary | Serve up on to bowls or plates, sprinkled with a little fresh coriander, desiccated coconut flakes and the finely sliced chilli

SWEET PEPPER FAJITAS

We challenged ourselves to create the ultimate healthy fajita and we think this combination of peppers, beans, guacamole and salsa hits the spot. It's a delicious Spanish-inspired fried pepper recipe that works really well as part of a hybrid fajita platter that would please a crowd. It's great as a lunch, dinner or even in a packed lunch!

MAKES 6 LARGE FAJITAS

olive oil, for frying
1 onion
2 garlic cloves
6 mixed red, yellow and green peppers
½ tbsp dark brown sugar
1 tsp hot chilli powder
1 tsp ground cumin
1 tsp paprika
¼ tsp cayenne pepper
¼ tsp garlic powder
a pinch of black pepper
1 x 400g tin kidney beans
30g fresh coriander leaves
1 x 400g tin refried beans, optional
1 x portion Perfectly Boiled Rice
    (see page 207) or one packet of
    pre-cooked rice
1 x portion Guacamole (shop-bought
    or see page 194)
1 x portion Salsa (shop-bought or
    see page 195)
6 large tortillas
3 limes
50g tortilla chips
salt and black pepper

Preheat the oven to 150°C | Large frying pan on a medium heat

Add a little oil to the frying pan | Peel and finely slice the onion and garlic and add them to the pan | Cut the peppers in half, cut out the stems and seeds, slice the flesh into 5mm strips and add them to the pan | Sprinkle over the brown sugar and a pinch of salt

Put the chilli powder into a small bowl with the cumin, paprika, cayenne pepper, garlic powder and a pinch each of salt and pepper | Stir to mix and then tip over the peppers in the pan | Reduce the heat a little, then cook for 30 minutes until soft, stirring regularly so that the peppers don't stick to the pan

Meanwhile, drain the kidney beans and tip them into a serving bowl | Chop a third of the coriander leaves and add them to the kidney beans | Spoon the refried beans, if using, into another bowl | Tip the cooked rice into another bowl | Spoon the guacamole and salsa into separate serving bowls

Put the tortillas on to an ovenproof plate or baking tray, cover with foil and put in the oven to warm

The peppers are ready when they look well fried (but not blackened), are soft and taste sweet and delicious | Transfer them to a serving bowl | Take the tortillas out of the oven and transfer them to a serving plate

Cut the limes into quarters | Roughly chop the remaining coriander leaves | Fill a bowl with the tortilla chips

Take all the separate bowls to the table | Fill the fajitas with delicious dollops of everything and roll them up to enjoy!

THAI RED CURRY

Thai Red Curry may possibly be the best thing humans ever invented, at least since tools, the wheel and (maybe) sliced bread. It's a feel-good meal with a hell of a kick. It's always best when you make your own paste; it doesn't take long and you can keep half for Tom Yum Soup (see page 63) or freeze it for later.

SERVES 4

1 red pepper
1 green pepper
1 fresh red chilli
200g mushrooms
60g baby corn
2 tbsp vegetable oil
1 x 400ml tin coconut milk
150ml vegetable stock
1 tbsp palm sugar (or regular sugar)
2 tbsp agave syrup
4 tbsp soy sauce
160g baby plum tomatoes
50g mangetout
½ x 425g tin lychees, optional

FOR THE THAI RED CURRY PASTE
(MAKES 300G)
1 tsp cumin seeds
2 tbsp coriander seeds
2cm piece fresh ginger
5 shallots
5 garlic cloves
2 lemongrass stalks
3 fresh red chillies
1 red bird's eye chilli, optional
1 tsp black peppercorns
½ roasted red pepper from a jar
2 tbsp tomato purée
3 kaffir lime leaves
½ lime
10g fresh coriander, plus extra
    for garnish
2 tsp salt
50ml water

Liquidiser | Large deep frying pan or wok on a high heat

To make the Thai red curry paste, scatter the cumin and coriander seeds over the pan and toast for 2 minutes | Peel the ginger by scraping off the skin with a spoon and roughly chop | Peel and roughly chop the shallots | Peel the garlic | Trim and roughly chop the lemongrass | Rip the stems from the chillies, removing the seeds if you prefer a milder sauce

Put the toasted seeds into the liquidiser along with the ginger, shallots, garlic and lemongrass | Add the fresh red chillies, bird's eye chilli, if using, peppercorns, roasted red pepper, tomato purée and the lime leaves | Squeeze in the lime juice, catching any pips in your other hand | Add the 10g fresh coriander, salt and a splash of water, then whizz until really smooth with no bits, adding up to 50ml of water to loosen it if necessary | Spoon 100g of the paste into a bowl and set the rest aside to use another time (freeze it in batches of 100g)

Cut the red and green peppers in half and cut out the stems and seeds, then cut into 2cm chunks | Rip the stems from 2 of the chillies, removing the seeds if you prefer a milder flavour, and cut into slices | Slice the mushrooms and halve the baby corn

Put the pan back on a high heat and add the oil | When it's hot, add the 100g curry paste and fry for 2 minutes, until the paste deepens in colour and smells amazing | Pour in the coconut milk and vegetable stock and stir well to mix everything together | Add the sugar, agave syrup, soy sauce, peppers, chilli, mushroom, baby corn, tomatoes and mangetout | Drain the lychees, if using and add them to the pan | Bring to the boil and simmer for 7–10 minutes, until the vegetables are cooked through | Taste and adjust the seasoning, adding salt, sugar or agave syrup as required

Spoon the curry into bowls, garnish with a handful of coriander leaves and serve alongside white rice

RED RATATOUILLE RISOTTO

Sometimes ideas hide in plain sight: we thought to ourselves, why couldn't we use red wine to make risotto? This controversial idea has upset some but pleased many more, with hundreds of people recreating this dish and sending us their pictures. It has all the goodness of risotto but with the romantic flair of red wine.

SERVES 4

1 aubergine (about 250g)
1 courgette (about 200g)
6 tomatoes (about 460g)
4 tbsp olive oil
1 large red onion
2 garlic cloves
5 sun-dried tomatoes in oil (about 50g)
2 sprigs fresh rosemary
2 sprigs fresh thyme
900ml vegetable stock
2 tbsp tomato purée
225g risotto rice
125ml red wine
1½ tbsp dairy-free butter
2 tbsp pine nuts, to serve
handful fresh basil leaves, to serve
salt and black pepper

Preheat oven to 180°C | Line a baking tray | Medium saucepan on a low heat | Medium saucepan on a medium heat

Trim the aubergine, courgette and tomatoes and cut them into 2½cm chunks | Put them all on the lined baking tray, drizzle over 2 tablespoons of the oil and season with salt and pepper | Put the tray in the oven and bake for 40 minutes

Meanwhile, peel and finely chop the red onion and garlic | Finely chop the sun-dried tomatoes | Remove the leaves from the herbs by running your thumb and forefinger from the top to the base of the stems (the leaves should easily come away), then finely chop

Place the stock in the medium saucepan on a low heat and keep warm

Warm the remaining 2 tablespoons of oil in the other pan | Add the chopped red onion to the pan and cook until soft and translucent, about 10–15 minutes | Add the garlic and cook for a further 1 minute | Add the rosemary and thyme, sun-dried tomatoes and tomato purée and give everything a stir | Cook for another 4–5 minutes

Pour the risotto rice into the pan and stir it around for 1 minute | Increase the heat slightly, pour in the red wine and stir until the rice has absorbed all the wine | Now start adding the stock, a ladleful at a time, waiting until the stock has been absorbed before adding another ladleful (you might not need all of it)

After 15 minutes, the rice should be about 2–3 minutes away from being perfectly al dente | Take the roasted ratatouille vegetables out of the oven, scrape them into the pan and fold them into the risotto along with all their juices | Stir until the rice is just cooked | Remove the pan from the heat and add the dairy-free butter | Season with salt and pepper

Divide between 4 bowls | Sprinkle over the pine nuts and garnish with fresh basil leaves

SAAG ALOO CURRY

This is definitely one of our healthier curries, but it's also powerfully spicy and tastes like a takeaway at home. There are lots of layers of flavour, the fenugreek being the star. We've made our spinach three ways to get maximum creaminess and freshness. Serve this with a couple of other curries for a DIY Indian sensation.

SERVES 2–4

FOR THE POTATOES
450g new potatoes
1 white onion
3 garlic cloves
2 tbsp sunflower oil
¼ tsp cumin seeds
1 tsp turmeric
2 tsp garam masala
½ tsp salt

FOR THE CURRY
1 white onion
1 fresh chilli
2 garlic cloves
6cm piece fresh ginger
2 medium tomatoes (about 175g)
400g baby leaf spinach
75ml water
2 tbsp sunflower oil
2 tbsp garam masala
1 tsp turmeric
1 tbsp ground coriander
1 tsp ground fenugreek
1 tsp salt, plus a little extra
½ tsp sugar
100ml soy cream
½ lemon

Medium saucepan of boiling salted water on a high heat | Large frying pan on a medium heat | Liquidiser | Deep frying pan with a lid on a medium heat

Peel the potatoes and cut them all in half | Put them into the medium saucepan and add just enough water to cover | Put the pan on a high heat and bring to the boil, then immediately reduce the heat to medium and simmer until cooked, about 12–15 minutes | Take the pan off the heat and drain the potatoes through a colander

Meanwhile, peel and finely chop the onion | Peel and mince the garlic | Add the oil to the large frying pan on a medium heat | Sprinkle in the cumin seeds and stir until they release their aroma, about 1 minute

Add the chopped onion and garlic and stir until the onion has softened, about 15 minutes | Add the potatoes, the turmeric, garam masala and salt | Stir until the potatoes have taken on the colour of the spices | Remove from the heat and set aside

Peel and finely dice the onion for the curry | Rip the stem from the chilli, cut it in half lengthways (remove the seeds for a milder sauce), then finely chop | Peel and mince the garlic | Peel the ginger by scraping off the skin with a spoon and finely chop | Finely chop the tomatoes

Roughly chop 100g of the spinach and finely chop another 100g | Put the remaining 200g spinach into the liquidiser with the water and whizz until completely blended

Add the oil to the deep frying pan | Scrape in the chopped onions and garlic and fry until soft, about 10–15 minutes | Add the chilli and ginger and stir for 2 more minutes | Add the tomatoes and stir until softened, about 3–5 minutes | Add the garam masala and turmeric, the ground coriander, fenugreek, salt and sugar and stir until well combined

Add the roughly chopped spinach and stir until completely wilted | Add the finely chopped spinach and stir to mix | Pour in the blended spinach and stir to until you have a dark green sauce | Simmer until thickened, about 10 minutes

Pour in the soy cream and tip in the potatoes | Stir to cover the potatoes and the sauce is bubbling slightly | Squeeze over the juice of the lemon, catching any pips in your other hand | Serve hot alongside rice or naan

SHEPHERD'S POTATO

This is our (slightly ridiculous) remix of two British classics: shepherd's pie and jacket potato. We've turned them on their heads to create possibly the poshest jacket potato you will ever eat. The hearty, smoky, filling mince and fluffy potato goodness create a night-in dish to impress.

MAKES 6

6 large baking potatoes
2 tbsp olive oil, plus a little bit extra
1 white onion
1 celery stick
1 medium carrot
2 garlic cloves
3 sprigs fresh rosemary, plus extra
    to serve
3 sprigs fresh thyme
2 tsp wholegrain mustard
3 tbsp tomato purée
1 tbsp soy sauce
150g chestnut mushrooms
120g cooked puy lentils (home-made
    or from a packet)
250ml vegetable stock
1½ tbsp dairy-free butter
2 tbsp nutritional yeast
1 tsp chilli flakes, to serve
salt and black pepper

Preheat the oven to 200°C | Baking tray | Deep frying pan on a medium heat

Put the potatoes on the baking tray and prick them with a fork | Drizzle with the 2 tablespoons of olive oil, season with salt and pepper, then rub them all over until completely covered | Put the tray in the hot oven and bake for 45–60 minutes, until soft

Peel and finely chop the white onion | Trim the leaves and root from the celery, then finely chop | Trim the carrot, peeling it if you like, and finely chop

Add a little oil to the hot pan | Add the chopped onions, celery and carrots and fry until they start to soften, about 5–10 minutes | Peel and crush the garlic into the pan | Remove the leaves from the rosemary and thyme by running your thumb and forefinger from the top to the base of the stems (the leaves should easily come away), finely chop and add to the pan | Season and cook for a further 2–3 minutes | Add the mustard, tomato purée and soy sauce and stir | Reduce the heat to a light simmer

Chop the mushrooms very finely and add them to the pan | Add the lentils, stir everything together and cook for 5–7 minutes | Pour in the stock and mix

When they're done, take the potatoes out of the oven and let them cool down for a few minutes | Use a sharp knife to cut a round lid off the top of each potato | Scoop out the fluffy middles, leaving at least a 1cm lining all round the insides, and transfer to a bowl | Add the dairy-free butter, nutritional yeast and a pinch of salt and pepper to the bowl and mash

Fill each potato to the brim with the mushroom mince and top with a large dollop of mashed potato | Put the tray in the oven and bake for 10–15 minutes to get the topping nice and crispy | Take the tray out of the oven | Sprinkle each potato with chilli flakes, the remaining chopped rosemary and some pepper before serving

SPAGHETTI BOLOGNESE

Could this be the world's favourite comfort meal? Our spag bol has all the deliciousness of the original, but with minced mushrooms providing the rich, smoky flavour. If you're looking for a warming, satisfying and healthy(ish) dinner, then look no further. Perfect for a date night and great with a glass of red wine.

SERVES 4–6

700g chestnut mushrooms
1 tbsp olive oil
500g spaghetti
a few small fresh basil leaves, to serve
salt and pepper

FOR THE TOMATO SAUCE
2 red onions
1 celery stick
4 garlic cloves
2 carrots
1 tbsp olive oil
1 tbsp tomato purée
300ml red wine
1 tsp balsamic vinegar
½ tbsp dried oregano
1 bay leaf
2 tsp soy sauce

Food processor | Large frying pan on a high heat | Large saucepan | Kettle boiled

Put the mushrooms in the food processor and pulse until very finely minced (you can chop them if you prefer, but it's quicker with a food processor)

Pour the oil into the frying pan | Add the mushrooms and season with a small pinch of salt and pepper | Cook for 10–15 minutes, stirring regularly, until all the liquid has evaporated and the mushrooms are well browned | Take the pan off the heat, transfer the mushrooms to a bowl and set aside

Peel and roughly chop the onions for the tomato sauce | Trim the leaves and root from the celery and roughly chop | Peel the garlic | Trim the carrots and peel if the skin is tough, then roughly chop | Put the chopped vegetables and garlic into the food processor and mince well

Put the same pan back on a medium-high heat and add the oil | Add the minced onions, garlic, carrots and celery and cook for about 10 minutes, until all the vegetables are soft | Stir in the tomato purée | Add the red wine, balsamic vinegar, oregano, bay leaf and soy sauce | Stir everything together and then turn down the heat | Simmer for 10 minutes

Meanwhile, put the large saucepan on a high heat, pour in the hot water, season with a big pinch of salt and bring to the boil | Add the pasta to the pan and cook until al dente, following the instructions on the packet | Spoon 100ml of the pasta water into a cup and set aside | Drain the pasta

Taste the sauce and season with salt and pepper | Add the minced mushrooms to the simmering sauce, turn up the heat and pour in the reserved pasta water | Stir everything together and let the sauce simmer for another 3–5 minutes to warm through

Pour the sauce into the pasta pot and stir everything together so that the sauce completely covers the pasta | Scatter over the basil leaves and grind over some black pepper | Serve to happy faces!

03

SHOW-PIECES

Now it's real wow-time
Create awesome showpieces
To impress your guests

BURRITO SAMOSAS

This two-dish combination is a BOSH! classic and an internet sensation. This is the traditional burrito ingredients in an unfamiliar but fantastic form. It's perfect for lunch, dinner or you can take it on the go with you. It's a hearty, full meal best served with salad and Guacamole (see page 194) or Salsa (see page 195).

MAKES 5

3 Maris Piper or other fluffy potatoes
    (about 500g)
1 red onion
3 garlic cloves
1 red pepper
1 fresh red chilli
3 tbsp vegetable oil
2 tsp smoked paprika
1 tbsp ground coriander
2 tsp ground cumin
1 tbsp + ½ tsp Tabasco sauce, or to taste
1 x 400g tin black beans
250g cooked basmati rice (shop-bought
    or Perfectly Boiled Rice, see page 207)
1½ limes
15g fresh coriander leaves
100g dairy-free cheese
6 large tortillas
Guacamole (shop-bought or
    see page 194), to serve
Salsa (shop-bought or see page 195),
    to serve
salt

Preheat oven to 180°C | Line a baking tray | Medium saucepan on a high heat | Large frying pan | Pastry brush

Peel the potatoes and chop them into 1cm chunks | Put them into the medium saucepan and add just enough water to cover | Put the pan on a high heat and bring to the boil, then immediately reduce the heat to medium and simmer until cooked, about 10 minutes | Take the pan off the heat and drain the potatoes through a colander

Meanwhile, peel and finely chop the red onion and garlic | Cut the pepper in half and cut out the stem and seeds, then finely chop | Rip the stem from the chilli, cut it in half lengthways and remove the seeds if you prefer a milder flavour, then finely chop

Put the large frying pan on a medium heat and add the vegetable oil | Once it's hot, add the minced vegetables and fry until soft, about 10 minutes | Add the smoked paprika, ground coriander, cumin, 1 tablespoon of the Tabasco and a pinch of salt to the pan and stir everything together | Add the potatoes to the pan and stir until they've taken on all the colours and flavours and begun to crisp up slightly on the sides, about 10 minutes | Drain the black beans and tip them into the pan | Stir until warmed through | Take the pan off the heat and transfer the contents to a mixing bowl

Tip the pre-cooked rice into a mixing bowl and fluff it with a fork | Cut the limes in half and squeeze over the juice, catching any pips in your other hand | Scatter over the coriander leaves, a pinch of salt and ½ teaspoon of the Tabasco and stir them into the rice

Grate the dairy-free cheese into a bowl

Take one of the tortillas and cut into 5 equal-sized triangles | Cut across the curved edge of each triangle so that you have three straight sides | Set aside these triangles, which will be used to seal your samosas

Take another tortilla and lay it out on a clean work surface | Take about one-fifth of the rice and place it in the centre of the tortilla | Follow with one-fifth of the dairy-free cheese and then one-fifth of the potato mixture | Shape the filling roughly into triangles with your hands, making sure it is in the middle of the tortilla | Place one of the tortilla triangles on top of the ingredients and press down slightly | Brush the rim of the round tortilla as well as the tortilla triangle with water (this will act as a glue to stick them together) | Fold the edges of the tortilla into the middle to form a triangle | Put the 'samosa' on the lined baking tray, fold side down | Repeat with the remaining samosas

Put the tray in the oven and bake for 20–25 minutes, until the samosas are crisp to the touch | Remove from the oven and serve with guacamole and salsa for happy dipping!

MASSAMAN CURRY

This is an absolute jaw-dropper of a curry. It has an incredible depth of hearty, umami-like flavour and a richness that keeps on giving. The spice kick is big but not too bold as it is infused throughout the dish. You could make this in the morning and leave it in the slow cooker all day for melt-in-your-mouth veggies. Serve with Perfectly Boiled Rice (see page 207).

SERVES 4

1 tsp fennel seeds
1 tsp cumin seeds
1 tsp coriander seeds
6 cloves
vegetable oil
2 lemongrass stalks
8 shallots
4 garlic cloves
2½cm piece fresh ginger
30g fresh coriander
3 kaffir lime leaves
2 tbsp chilli paste
1 x 400ml tin coconut milk
1 potato (about 225g)
2 sweet potatoes (about 500g)
1 red pepper
100g green beans
½ small cauliflower
500ml vegetable stock
1 tbsp tamarind paste
2 bay leaves
1 cinnamon stick
4 tbsp roasted peanuts
rice, to serve

Large saucepan on a high heat | Liquidiser

Put the fennel, cumin and coriander seeds and cloves into the saucepan and toast for about 2 minutes, until fragrant | Transfer to the liquidiser | Put the pan back on the heat and add a little oil

Trim the top and bottom off the lemongrass and carefully cut them in half lengthways | Peel the shallots and garlic | Peel the ginger by scraping off the skin with a spoon | Chop the leaves from the fresh coriander and set aside, reserving the stalks

Roughly chop the lemongrass, shallots, garlic and ginger and tip them into the pan | Fry for 3 minutes, until lightly browned, then tip into the liquidiser | Add the lime leaves, chilli paste and coriander stalks | Blend until you've created a completely smooth paste with a deep brown colour and no bits | Pour back into the pan, turn the heat up to medium-high and fry for 2 minutes, or until golden brown | Pour in the coconut milk, reduce the heat to medium and let it bubble away slowly until reduced by a third

Meanwhile, peel the potato and sweet potatoes and chop into 3cm cubes | Cut the pepper in half and cut out the stem and seeds, then chop into 3cm cubes along with the green beans | Break the cauliflower into small florets

Add the vegetable stock to the pan, followed by the potato, sweet potato, cauliflower, red pepper and green beans | Add the tamarind paste, bay leaves and cinnamon stick and bring to the boil, stirring continuously | Immediately reduce the heat to low and leave to simmer for 45–60 minutes, stirring occasionally, until you have a very thick, rich, curry consistency

Chop the reserved coriander leaves | Serve the curry alongside boiled rice, scattered with the roasted peanuts and fresh coriander

GIANT BURRITO CAKE

A giant burrito, wrapped up warm then baked in a saucepan = the most amazing sharing platter you ever had! Inspired by our good friends at Jungle Creations, this dish is incredibly easy and impressive. It's been cooked time and time again by our fans and is one of our finest food remixes to date. You can see this in all its flavour-packed glory on the next page.

SERVES 8–10

100g cherry tomatoes

3 spring onions

1 tbsp olive oil

6–7 large white tortillas

10 slices dairy-free cheese

1 lime

FOR THE VEGETABLE FILLING

2 medium sweet potatoes (about 500g)

2 tbsp olive oil

½–1 tsp chilli flakes

1 red onion

1 red pepper

1 yellow pepper

1 green pepper

1 tbsp olive oil

1 tsp garlic powder

1 tsp paprika

1½ tsp cayenne pepper

1 tsp onion powder

1 tsp ground cumin

salt and black pepper

FOR THE RICE FILLING

2 tbsp olive oil

5 spring onions

3 garlic cloves

250g cooked basmati rice (shop-bought or Perfectly Boiled Rice, see page 207)

1 x 400g tin black beans

¼ tsp Tabasco sauce

salt

1 tbsp ground cumin

25g fresh coriander

Preheat oven to 180°C | Line 2 baking trays | Large ovenproof frying pan | Medium saucepan | Pastry brush

To make the vegetable filling, first cut the sweet potatoes into 5mm thick slices | Lay them out on one of the lined baking trays, drizzle them with 1 tablespoon olive oil and sprinkle over the chilli flakes and a good pinch each of salt and pepper | Mix everything around so that the potatoes are well coated | Put the tray into the hot oven and bake for 30 minutes, then remove the tray and set it aside

While the potatoes are in the oven, peel and finely slice the red onion | Cut the peppers in half and cut out the stems and seeds then cut them into slices | Spread the onion and pepper slices over the second lined baking tray and drizzle them with the remaining oil | Sprinkle over the garlic powder, paprika, cayenne pepper, onion powder and ground cumin | Mix everything together and then put the tray into the oven below the potatoes to bake for 20 minutes, then remove the tray and set it aside

To prepare the rice filling, put the large frying pan on a medium heat and add 2 tablespoons of olive oil | Trim and finely slice the spring onions | Peel and finely slice the garlic | Put the sliced spring onions and garlic into the pan and stir them around until you've released the aroma of the garlic, this should take about 2–3 minutes | Tip in the pre-cooked rice | Drain the black beans and add them to the pan

Add the Tabasco sauce, a good pinch of salt and ground cumin to the pan and stir everything together, then take the pan off the heat | Pick the leaves from the coriander and add them to the pan, discarding the stalks or using them for something else | Stir everything together again | Tip the contents of the pan into a large serving bowl and then clean the pan ready to use again

Trim and finely chop the cherry tomatoes | Trim the spring onions and finely chop | Put the tomatoes and chopped spring onions into small bowls so that they are ready when you build your giant burrito cake

Now you're ready to put it all together and assemble your cake | Brush the frying pan with 1 tablespoon olive oil to stop the burrito cake sticking | Now arrange four of the tortillas around the edges of the pan as if you are laying out the petals of a flower and draping each one over the edges of the pan (if you are using a really big frying pan you might need one more tortilla to make sure your burrito cake will be completely sealed) | Press a final tortilla into the centre of the pan so that the base of the pan is completely covered and there are no gaps

Now you're going to fill your burrito cake | First spoon half the rice into the burrito base and spread it out evenly with the back of a wooden spoon | Place a layer of dairy-free cheese slices on top of the rice, followed by a layer of the sweet potato slices | Next, take half the onion and pepper slices and place them on top of the sweet potato to make an even layer | Sprinkle over half the chopped cherry tomatoes and half the sliced spring onions | Cut the lime in half and squeeze over the juice of one half, catching any pips in the other hand | Repeat with a layer of rice, dairy-free cheese slices, sweet potato slices, onion and pepper slices, cherry tomatoes, spring onions and the juice from the other half of the lime so that you use up all of the ingredients | Make sure the filling is nice and even and as round as possible as this will form the shape of your burrito cake

Lay the remaining tortilla over the top of the filling to form a lid | Use a pastry brush or your finger to wet the edges of each tortilla with a thin coating of water (this will act as a glue to stick the tortillas together and seal the cake) | Fold the overhanging tortillas neatly over the filling and into the middle of the cake, starting with one tortilla and working your way around the cake, and smooth them down to seal the cake

Put the pan into the hot oven and bake the burrito cake for 20 minutes, until the filling is cooked through, the tortilla casing is golden and the cake looks nice and solid | Take the pan out of the oven

To serve your burrito cake, place a large serving board on top of the pan and very carefully flip both the pan and board over to release the cake | Use a sharp knife to cut it into neat slices and enjoy your giant burrito cake!

MEZZE CAKE

This is one of the finest dishes we've ever made or eaten, with every mouthful the perfect combination of flavours you could hope to get in a Middle Eastern restaurant. It's a proud remix of an entire cuisine into a cake and, while it is a bit of a labour of love, it's guaranteed to excite your taste buds. Check out the photo on the next page for inspiration!

SERVES 8–10

2 aubergines

2 courgettes

olive oil

1 thin flatbread (under 5mm)

300g Hummus (shop-bought or see page 199)

2–3 tbsp chilli sauce

18–20 sun-dried tomatoes

100g Olive Tapenade (shop-bought or see page 192)

250g cooked basmati rice (shop-bought or Perfectly Boiled Rice, see page 207)

7 roasted red peppers from a jar

8 artichokes from a jar

100g Baba Ganoush (shop-bought or see page 193)

FOR THE FALAFEL MIX

1 x 400g tin chickpeas

1 small red onion

15g fresh parsley leaves

10g fresh coriander leaves

2 tsp garlic powder

1½–2 tsp ground cumin

1½–2 tsp ground coriander

2 tsp harissa paste

2 tbsp plain flour

1 tbsp olive oil

salt

Preheat oven to 180°C | Baking tray drizzled with olive oil | 20cm deep loose-bottomed or springform cake tin | Food processor | Griddle pan

Cut off the stems of the aubergines and cut the flesh into slices about 5mm thick | Trim the courgettes and cut them into 5mm slices | Set aside three of the nicest-looking slices of each (choose ones that are roughly the same size) | Spread the rest over the greased baking tray and drizzle them with a bit more oil | Rub the oil into the slices | Put the tray into the hot oven and roast for 30 minutes, until the vegetables are soft | Remove the tray from the oven and set it aside to cool

Next, place the flatbread on a chopping board and lay the round cake tin on top of it | Cut around the tin with a sharp knife to make a flatbread circle that will fit inside the bottom of it | Put the flatbread inside the tin and spread it with a 1cm layer of hummus | Drizzle a tablespoon of chilli sauce over the top of the hummus

You're now going to layer up the ingredients inside the tin to build up your mezze cake | First place a flat ring of sun-dried tomatoes all around the edge of the tin | Then, inside the ring of tomatoes, build another ring of roasted courgette slices, placing one in the centre if there is space | Fill in any gaps between the slices with spoonfuls of the olive tapenade

Next, spoon a layer of the pre-cooked rice over the vegetables so that it is about 5mm deep all over and press it down firmly with the back of the spoon to get it nice and firm and even all over | Place a layer of the roasted aubergine and courgette slices over the top of the rice layer and fill the gaps with more blobs of the olive tapenade | Once again, press down all over the top of the cake with a spoon to keep it all nice and compact (this step is important as it will hold the cake together when it cooks and ensure you get immaculate slices)

Cut the roasted peppers into 2cm strips and arrange them in a star shape over the top of the cake and fill the spaces in between the star with pieces of artichoke | Firm everything down again with the back of a spoon | Arrange more of the roasted courgettes around the edge of the tin and place some sun-dried tomatoes in the space in the middle | Fill in the gaps with spoonfuls of the baba ganoush

Next prepare the falafel topping | Drain the chickpeas and tip them into the food processor | Peel the onion and roughly chop it, then add it to the chickpeas | Throw in the fresh parsley and coriander leaves, the garlic powder, the ground cumin, ground coriander and the harissa paste | Spoon the flour into the food processor with the tablespoon of olive oil and pinch of salt | Whizz everything together until you have a thick paste | Spoon the falafel mixture all over the top of the cake and smooth it out using the back of the spoon or a palette knife as if you were icing a cake, until you have an even 1cm layer

Put the cake in the hot oven and bake for 20–25 minutes, until the falafel on the top has hardened and everything is cooked through

While the cake is cooking, put the griddle pan on a medium-high heat and drizzle it with some olive oil | Heat the oil until it's really hot | Put the reserved slices of aubergine and courgette into the hot pan and cook them on one side until they have defined char lines and are softened, then flip them over to cook the other side (try not to move them around too much in the pan as we want to make nice neat black griddle lines), the aubergines will take around 5 minutes per side and the courgettes will take about 3–4 minutes per side | Remove the pan from the heat and transfer the slices to a plate

When the cake is ready, take it out of the oven | To finish and decorate it, spoon the remaining hummus on top and spread it out neatly until you have a 5mm–1cm layer all over the top of the cake | Now make it look pretty by decorating it with the griddled aubergine and courgette slices and then drizzling it all over the top with the rest of the chilli sauce | Finally, scatter over the fresh green coriander leaves

Carefully release the cake from the tin and reveal your masterpiece | You'll need to use a very sharp knife to slice the cake and serve it immediately | If the knife gets caught at any point, a sharp pair of scissors can help you to cut it more neatly | Pay attention to making sure the flatbread at the bottom is completely cut through before you remove the slice so that everything comes out in one perfect tidy piece!

ULTIMATE CHILLI

This deep, dark and smoky chilli is perhaps the richest we've tasted. The flavour comes from the mushroom base, but is boosted by untraditional ingredients like soy sauce, balsamic vinegar, maple syrup and chocolate. You should absolutely leave it bubbling away if you have the time. It's so, so good – you'll be bowled over by the end result. Turn the page for a mouthwatering preview.

SERVES 6

400g mushrooms
olive oil
¼ tsp salt
¼ tsp black pepper
2 red onions
4 garlic cloves
2 fresh red chillies
30g fresh coriander
1 celery stick
1 red pepper
1 tbsp tomato purée
250ml red wine
2 tsp soy sauce
1 tsp balsamic vinegar
2 x 400g tins chopped tomatoes
1 x 400g tin black beans
1 x 400g tin kidney beans
1½ tsp maple syrup
10g dark chocolate

FOR THE SPICE MIX
1 tsp chilli powder
1 tsp ground cumin
1 tsp smoked paprika
½ tsp ground cinnamon
½ tsp dried oregano
½ tsp salt
½ tsp black pepper
1 bay leaf

Food processor | Frying pan on a medium-high heat | Large saucepan on a medium heat

Put the mushrooms in the food processor and pulse until very finely minced (you can chop them if you prefer, but it's quicker and better with a food processor)

Pour a little oil into the hot frying pan | Once the oil is hot, tip in the mushrooms with the salt and pepper and cook for 5 minutes | Take the pan off the heat, transfer the mushrooms to a bowl and set aside

Peel and mince the red onions | Peel and mince the garlic | Rip the stems from the chillies, cut them in half lengthways and remove the seeds if you prefer a milder sauce, then chop finely | Remove the leaves from the coriander and set aside | Finely chop the stalks | Trim the leaves and root from the celery | Cut the pepper in half and cut out the stem and seeds | Cut the celery and pepper into very small chunks

Add a little oil to the large saucepan | Once it is hot, add the minced onions and garlic, the finely chopped coriander stalks and the chillies and cook gently for 5–10 minutes, making sure you stir constantly | Add the chopped celery and red pepper chunks to the pan and stir

Add all the spice mix ingredients to the pan and stir so that the spices are well mixed and coat all the vegetables | Stir in the tomato purée to give a rich colour and depth of flavour | Pour the red wine, soy sauce and balsamic vinegar into the pan and turn up the heat to high | Stir constantly until the liquid has reduced by two-thirds and the alcoholic aroma has subsided | Tip the chopped tomatoes into the pan, stir into the chilli and simmer for 5 minutes, until the sauce is noticeably thicker

Drain the black beans and kidney beans and add them to the pan along with the maple syrup, dark chocolate and the minced mushrooms | Stir everything together really well and then reduce the heat to a very gentle simmer | Leave this bubbling away with the lid off, stirring occasionally until it's reduced to the right thickness (at least 10 minutes) | You can leave it bubbling for longer to deepen the flavours, adding more water if needed to keep the right consistency

Take the lid off the pan and remove the bay leaf | Stir the coriander leaves into the chilli and serve – or make Big Bad Nachos!

BIG BAD NACHOS

Shortly after the first chilli came the first nachos. We're massive chilli fans, but we always have loads left over and these nachos are a brilliant way to use it up. This dish is a sure-fire movie night crowd-pleaser. Feel free to adjust the quantities and experiment with soy cream, coconut yoghurt, fresh chillies or refried beans – see overleaf for serving inspiration.

SERVES 8

2 x 200g bags tortilla chips
1 x 200g jar jalapeño chillies
50g dairy-free cheese such as our Garlic & Herb Cashew Cheese (see page 210), optional
1 x portion Ultimate Chilli (see opposite) or leftovers from a previous meal
1 x portion Guacamole (shop-bought or see page 194)
1 x portion Salsa (shop-bought or see page 195)
handful fresh coriander leaves

Preheat oven to 200°C | Large ovenproof dish (about 30 x 23cm)

Tip the tortilla chips into the ovenproof dish so that they cover the bottom | Slice the jalapeños and scatter them over the nachos | Throw in the dairy-free cheese, if using | Cover with the Ultimate Chilli

Put the dish in the oven and bake until the tortilla chips have started to brown and the chilli is heated through, about 10–15 minutes | Take the dish out of the oven

Dot random spots of guacamole and salsa over the top | Chop up the coriander leaves and scatter them over the nachos

PERFECT PIZZA

Pizza, pizza. The perfect sharing food. It's satisfying, filling and can be a healthy(ish) choice when it's done right. People are often afraid of dough-making but it doesn't take long and the kneading is incredibly satisfying, maybe even meditative. Make double and you can freeze half for next time. We recommend a pizza stone for a really good base.

BASIC PIZZA DOUGH

MAKES 2 LARGE PIZZA BASES

500g strong bread flour
3½g fast-action dried yeast
1½ tsp salt
340ml water, at room temperature

Clean work surface dusted liberally with flour

Measure the flour into a large bowl | Stir in the yeast and salt and mix it all together well | Use your hands to make a well in the middle of the bowl | Pour in the water and slowly mix together, kneading well with your fingers | When a dough has come together, bring it out of the bowl and put it on the floured work surface | Knead for 15 minutes, stretching and folding the dough, turning it 90 degrees and then repeating until it becomes really smooth and springy | Wipe any flour or dough out of the bowl and rub the inside lightly with oil | Put the dough back in, cover with cling film and leave to rise for about 1 hour until doubled in size

Tip the risen dough back on to the work surface and give it another 60 seconds of kneading, then divide it into two | Cover each half with cling film and leave to prove for another 30 minutes | You can store the dough in cling film in the freezer for up to 1 month, defrosting completely before using

MIDDLE EAST PIZZA

With its Middle Eastern vibes, this pizza is a clear winner on pizza night. Feel free to play around with the ingredients. We use lots of jarred ingredients so it's a great store-cupboard standby. Serve alongside hummus, tapenade and any other mezze dishes you can think of!

MAKES 2 LARGE PIZZAS

flour, for dusting

1 x portion Basic Pizza Dough
    (see page 107)

semolina, for dusting

4 x artichoke hearts preserved in oil
    (from a jar)

1 red pepper preserved in oil (from a jar)

6 cherry tomatoes

6 sun-dried tomatoes

½ red onion

75g Hummus (shop-bought or
    see page 199), plus extra to serve

50g Olive Tapenade (shop-bought or
    see page 192), plus extra to serve

handful fresh coriander, to serve

hot sauce, to serve

FOR THE TOMATO SAUCE

1 garlic clove

small handful fresh basil or 1 tsp dried

1 tbsp olive oil

200g tinned chopped tomatoes

1 tsp red wine vinegar

Preheat oven to 250°C | Pizza stone or heavy baking sheet heating up in the oven | Baking sheet dusted liberally with semolina | Clean work surface dusted liberally with flour | Liquidiser | Rolling pin (or use a clean, dry wine bottle)

First make the tomato sauce | Peel the garlic clove and add it to the liquidiser with the basil | Add the olive oil, tinned tomatoes and red wine vinegar | Whizz until really smooth

Tip one of the dough balls on to the floured work surface and roll it out to about 30cm diameter | Carefully transfer to the baking sheet, laying it over the semolina | Spoon a thin layer of tomato sauce over the top of the pizza, spreading it all the way to the edges | Set aside

Take your artichoke hearts out of the jar and cut them in half | Take the pepper out of the jar and wipe off any excess oil, then cut into thin strips | Halve the cherry tomatoes and sun-dried tomatoes | Peel and finely slice the onion

Decorate your pizza base with half the vegetables you've just prepared, making sure you leave a little space around them | Slide the base on to the hot pizza stone or baking sheet in the oven and bake for 10 minutes | Meanwhile prepare the second pizza

Remove the cooked pizza from the oven and spoon about 8 small dollops each of hummus and tapenade around the pizza, as artfully as you can | Chop the coriander leaves and sprinkle over the top, then splash over a few drops of hot sauce | Repeat with the second pizza and serve

AVOCADO TOAST PIZZA

This is the ultimate hipster dish and works as a brunch as much as a main. Think of a really good garlic bread pizza with a big power-up of avocado and delicious coriander and lemon zest.

MAKES 2 LARGE PIZZAS

1 garlic clove
1 fresh red chilli
30g fresh coriander
flour, for dusting
1 x portion Basic Pizza Dough
   (see page 107)
semolina, for dusting
3 tbsp olive oil
6 avocados
1 lemon
1–2 tsp chilli flakes
salt and black pepper
tomato salsa, for dipping, optional

Preheat oven to 250°C | Pizza stone or heavy baking sheet heating up in the oven | Rolling pin (or use a clean, dry wine bottle) | Baking sheet dusted liberally with semolina | Pastry brush

Peel and finely chop the garlic | Rip the stem from the chilli, cut it in half lengthways, remove the seeds if you prefer a milder flavour, and finely chop | Cut the stalks from the coriander and finely chop, reserving the leaves

Dust a clean, dry work surface liberally with flour | Roll out one of the dough balls to about 30cm diameter | Carefully transfer to the baking sheet, laying it over the semolina | Brush the top of the pizza with half the olive oil | Sprinkle half the garlic, chilli and chopped coriander stalks all over the pizza base | Carefully slide the pizza on to the hot pizza stone or baking sheet in the oven and cook for 10 minutes | Meanwhile, prepare the second base

Next prep the toppings | Halve and carefully stone the avocados by tapping the stone firmly with the heel of a knife so that it lodges in the pits, then twist and remove the stones | Run a dessert spoon around the inside of the skin to scoop out the avocado halves, then slice them finely, keeping the shape of the avocado halves

Slide the cooked pizza base on to a chopping board and put the second base in the oven

You're going to use 3 avocados for the first base | Pick up the first half of slices and lay it on the pizza, then press down gently to fan out the slices neatly | Repeat until the pizza is almost completely covered in avocado | Halve the lemon and squeeze one half all over the pizza, catching any pips in your other hand | Finely chop the coriander leaves and scatter half over the pizza | Season with salt and black pepper and sprinkle with chilli flakes

Remove the second base from the oven and repeat with the remaining toppings | Serve the pizzas on their own or with a tomato salsa for dipping, if using

JERK JACKFRUIT & PLANTAIN PIZZA

This evolved from our Reggae Reggae Pizza. We decided to badboy it up with spicy jerk jackfruit offset by sweet plantain. It's got a satisfying bite and comes fully loaded – this is a HOT pizza. Adjust the chillies to taste and add BBQ or jerk sauce for dipping.

MAKES 2 LARGE PIZZAS

1 x portion Basic Pizza Dough
(see page 107)
flour, for dusting
semolina, for dusting
2 tbsp olive oil
1 x 400g tin young green jackfruit
in spring water
1 ripe plantain (the skin should be
more black than yellow)
BBQ or jerk sauce, to serve, optional

FOR THE JERK SAUCE
1 fresh Scotch bonnet chilli
2 garlic cloves
5–7 sprigs fresh thyme
1 tsp ground cloves
1 tsp ground cinnamon
1 tsp ground nutmeg
2 tsp ground allspice
black pepper
olive oil

FOR THE TOMATO SAUCE
200g tinned chopped tomatoes
handful fresh basil or 1 tsp dried
1 garlic clove
1 tbsp olive oil
1 tsp red wine vinegar

Preheat oven to 250°C | Pizza stone or heavy baking sheet heating up in the oven | Liquidiser | Rolling pin (or use a clean, dry wine bottle) | Baking sheet dusted liberally with semolina | Large frying pan

First make the jerk sauce by ripping the stem from the chilli, cutting it in half lengthways and removing the seeds if you prefer a milder sauce, then finely chop | Peel and mince the garlic | Remove the leaves from the thyme by running your thumb and forefinger from the top to the base of the stems (the leaves should easily come away) and finely chop | Put the chilli, garlic, thyme, cloves, cinnamon, nutmeg and allspice in a mixing bowl with some black pepper and a dash of olive oil | Mix well

Take 1 tablespoon of the jerk sauce and put it into the liquidiser with the ingredients for the tomato sauce | Whizz until really smooth

Dust a clean, dry work surface liberally with flour | Roll out one of the dough balls to about 30cm diameter | Carefully transfer to the baking sheet, laying it over the semolina | Spoon a thin layer of tomato sauce over the top, spreading it all the way to the edges | Set aside

Put 1 tablespoon of oil into the frying pan and put it on a medium heat | Drain the jackfruit and cut into thin slices, following the grain of the fruit from the bottom to the top | Add to the jerk marinade and stir to coat | You can leave to marinate for an hour for a deeper flavour, or add straight to the hot pan and fry for 5 minutes, stirring regularly | Remove from the heat and transfer half the fruit to the pizza

Put the remaining oil into the pan and put it back on the heat | Peel and finely slice the plantain | Add to the pan and sauté for 3–5 minutes, turning a couple of times, until golden brown | Take off the heat and add half the slices to the pizza

Carefully slide the pizza on to the hot pizza stone or baking sheet and cook for 10 minutes | Meanwhile, assemble the second pizza

Remove the cooked pizza from the oven and follow with the second | Serve with BBQ or jerk sauce, if using

PETTIGREW'S PAELLA

This Spanish classic is loved by many, mastered by few. However, Henry's father has had a good crack and passed the recipe down proudly from father to son. Paella should never be stirred – unlike risotto, the rice needs to stay firm and not sticky. The lemon wedges served on every plate to be squeezed over before eating are absolutely non-negotiable! Turn over the page to see this in all its glory.

SERVES 4–6

1 large red pepper
200g tinned butter beans
1 small onion
1 large garlic clove
1 medium tomato (about 115g)
150g fine green beans
10 sprouting broccoli stems
200g tinned artichoke hearts
generous pinch of saffron
2 tbsp olive oil
1 tbsp paprika
½ tsp ground turmeric
1 litre good-quality vegetable stock
280g paella rice
1–2 lemons
salt and black pepper

Grill on high, or griddle on the highest heat | Baking tray | Large frying or paella pan | Pestle and mortar (or use a mug and teaspoon) | Kettle boiled | Clean tea towels

Cut the pepper in half and cut out the stem and seeds | Lay the pieces on the baking tray under a hot grill, skin side up (or on a hot griddle, skin side down) and heat until the skin blackens | Transfer to a plastic bag and seal inside | Leave to cool, then remove and remove the skin | Cut the flesh into 1½cm strips

Meanwhile, drain the butter beans | Peel and finely chop the onion and garlic | Finely chop the tomato | Trim the green beans and cut off the heads of the broccoli | Cut the beans and broccoli stems only into 1–2cm pieces | Quarter the artichoke hearts | Set all the chopped veggies aside for later

Put the saffron threads in the dry frying or paella pan and place it on a medium heat | Let it warm for about 1 minute to dry the saffron, then transfer to a mortar | Add a generous pinch of salt and pound with the pestle to grind them together

Add 1 tablespoon of the oil to the pan along with the red pepper | Cook for 10–15 minutes, turning occasionally, until the peppers are soft but not browned | Remove from the pan and set aside about 6 strips | Cut the rest into 1–2cm pieces

Add the onion to the pan along with the remaining tablespoon oil | Cook for 10–15 minutes, until the onion has softened and browned a little, stirring occasionally | Add the garlic and cook for a further 2 minutes | Add the tomato and cook for about 10 minutes more, stirring from time to time, until the tomato pieces turn mushy | Stir in the salty saffron threads, paprika, turmeric and a generous pinch of black pepper | Add the stock to the pan, turn up the heat and bring to the boil, then reduce the heat to medium

Stir in the green beans, butter beans, artichoke and red pepper pieces (reserving the strips) | Increase the heat to bring the pan back to a simmer, then lower to medium | Taste the paella liquid – it should have a good 'stock' taste that's a little too salty, so add a little more salt to the pan if necessary

Sprinkle the rice evenly over the pan | Bring it back to the boil, then reduce the heat to a fast simmer (medium-high) | Continue to simmer for 5 minutes without stirring | If you are using a large pan on a smaller burner you may need to move the pan around on the burner occasionally so that the rice cooks evenly across the pan

Decorate the surface of the paella with the red pepper strips and broccoli florets | Continue to cook without stirring for 10 minutes | Turn the broccoli a few times so that it cooks through, and check that the rice is still evenly distributed – you might need to use a spoon to move the rice in the pan

After 10 minutes, test the rice by biting a few grains | They should be translucent but al dente | If the pan starts to dry out before the rice is cooked, add 100ml boiling water by drizzling it through a strainer over the surface of the mixture (don't just pour it in) | If there is a lot of liquid visible when the rice is nearly cooked, consider either spooning some off or turning up the heat (a little bit of burning at the bottom of the pan is not considered a bad thing – the Valencians call it 'socarrat', and treasure it)

Once the rice is cooked enough, give it a last short burst of heat to get any remaining liquid really bubbling, then turn off the heat and cover the top of the pan with foil and a couple of clean tea towels | Leave it for 10–15 minutes – this improves the taste and texture and allows the rice to absorb any excess stock | Cut the lemons into wedges and serve alongside the paella

THE BIG BOSH! BURGER

We do love a good burger, and creating a big, meaty tasting burger was high up on our list of priorities. This one gets its richness from sweet potatoes, black beans and a whole host of herbs. It's packed full of protein and the soft patty gives a good, filling bite. To make this even better, add a helping of Ultimate BBQ Coleslaw (page 148) to the top of the burger.

SERVES 6

400g sweet potatoes
1 onion
olive oil
250g pre-cooked brown rice
20g breadcrumbs
½ tsp salt
½ tsp black pepper
½ tsp ground cumin
½ tsp garlic powder
½ tsp smoked paprika
2 tbsp plain flour
1 x 400g tin black beans

TO SERVE
1 beef tomato
1 gem lettuce
1 large red onion
6 burger buns
6 tsp tomato ketchup
6 tsp vegan mayonnaise
12 slices gherkin
6 slices dairy-free cheese

Preheat oven to 200°C | Line a baking tray | Large frying pan on a medium heat | Food processor

Peel the sweet potatoes and cut them into 2cm cubes | Put them on the lined baking tray and bake for 30 minutes | Take them out of the oven and set aside

Meanwhile, peel and mince the onion | Pour a little oil into the frying pan | Put the onion in the pan and fry for 10–15 minutes, until very soft | Transfer the onion to a large bowl and wipe out the pan

Put the baked sweet potato in the food processor | Add the rice, breadcrumbs, salt, pepper, cumin, garlic powder, smoked paprika and flour | Drain the black beans and add them to the food processor, then whizz everything up to a thick paste | Scrape the paste into the bowl with the onions and mix everything together with a spoon

Add a little oil to the pan and put it on a medium-high heat | Divide the mixture into six and use your hands to mould them into patty shapes | Place the patties in the hot pan and fry for 3 minutes on each side, until golden

While the burgers are cooking, slice the beef tomato into 6 thin slices | Separate the leaves of the lettuce and peel and slice the onion into thin rings

Build your burgers by placing them inside the burger buns, topping with ketchup, vegan mayo and slices of tomato and gherkin, lettuce, red onion, and dairy-free cheese

RICH & CREAMY LASAGNE

This lasagne is easy enough to make and will impress your dinner guests no end. The béchamel is creamy as hell and as long as there are no overlaps, the pasta will cook to perfection. This is perfect dinner-party fodder, or a treat for you and your loved one that will leave lots of leftovers – it may be even better the next day. Check out the photo on the next page.

SERVES 8

1 butternut squash (about 1kg)
3 medium aubergines (about 750g)
1 tsp chilli powder
4 tbsp olive oil, plus extra for greasing
3 tbsp balsamic vinegar
600g baby leaf spinach
500g dried pasta sheets
a few sprigs fresh rosemary, to serve

FOR THE TOMATO SAUCE
30g dried porcini mushrooms
4 tbsp olive oil
1 red onion
5 garlic cloves
1 carrot
2 celery sticks
1 red pepper
3 sprigs fresh rosemary
150ml red wine
2 x 400g tins chopped tomatoes
1 tsp caster sugar
salt and black pepper

FOR THE BÉCHAMEL
100g cashews
1 garlic clove
450ml plant-based milk
50g dairy-free butter
25g plain flour
25g nutritional yeast, optional
2 tsp onion powder
½ lemon
100ml water
salt and black pepper

Preheat oven to 180°C | Line 2 large baking trays | Brush the inside of a 25 x 35cm lasagne dish with oil | Kettle boiled | Large deep frying pan or casserole pan on a medium heat | Food processor, optional | Large saucepan with lid | Small saucepan | Medium saucepan | Liquidiser

....

Put the porcini mushrooms for the tomato sauce into a large mug and cover with boiling water, then set aside

Peel the squash, cut it in half and scoop out and discard the seeds | Trim the aubergines and cut the squash and aubergine into 1cm slices | Put them in a bowl with the chilli powder and 3 tablespoons of the olive oil and toss to coat | Lay the squash on one lined tray, the aubergine on the other | Put both trays in the oven and roast for 45 minutes

Meanwhile, make the tomato sauce | Heat the olive oil in the large deep frying pan or casserole pan | Peel and finely dice the onion and add it to the pan to soften for 3 minutes | Peel and mince the garlic, add to the pan and cook for a further 3 minutes

Trim and roughly chop the carrot and celery | Cut the pepper in half and cut out the stem and seeds | Remove the leaves from the rosemary sprigs by running your thumb and forefinger from the top to the base of the stems (the leaves should easily come away) | Put the carrot, celery, pepper and rosemary leaves in the food processor and pulse a few times until all the veg are finely chopped (or do this by hand)

Add the chopped veg to the pan with the onion and garlic | Stir and cook for 15 minutes | Pour in the red wine, increase the heat to medium-high and cook for a further 5–7 minutes, until the wine has cooked off but left everything a lovely red colour

Take the porcini out of the mug and finely chop | Add to the pan with the liquid from the mug, the chopped tomatoes and the sugar | Stir and simmer for a further 10 minutes

Remove the trays from the oven | Drizzle the aubergine with the balsamic vinegar and mix well | If the butternut squash is very wet, drain it in a sieve, pressing out the liquid | Transfer to a large bowl and quickly mash

Add the aubergine to the tomato sauce and simmer for a further 20 minutes, stirring occasionally, until the sauce has thickened | Taste and season with salt and pepper | Take off the heat and set aside

Put the remaining 1 tablespoon oil into the large saucepan and place it on a medium heat | Add the spinach and cover with a lid | Cook for about 5 minutes until wilted | Transfer to a sieve and squeeze out as much liquid as you can (or place in a clean tea towel and wring it out)

Now make the béchamel | Put a small saucepan of water on a high heat and bring to the boil | Add the cashews and boil for 10 minutes | Peel and mince the garlic

Put a medium saucepan on a medium heat | Warm the plant-based milk in the microwave | Put the dairy-free butter in the pan and stir with a wooden spoon until it melts, then turn the heat right down and gradually add the flour, stirring vigorously until you have a doughy paste | Gradually pour in the warm plant-based milk, stirring all the time until you have a thick, creamy sauce | Keep stirring until the sauce thickens to the consistency of custard | Add the garlic, nutritional yeast, if using, onion powder, plus a pinch of salt and pepper | Squeeze in the lemon juice, catching any pips with your other hand | Stir to mix together

Drain the cashews and rinse with cold water | Put them into the liquidiser with the 100ml water | Blend to a fine cream with no bits | Pour the béchamel into the liquidiser and blend everything together

Cover the base of the greased lasagne dish with pasta sheets, breaking them if necessary to make a complete and unbroken layer that will seal in the steam and properly cook the pasta | Spoon a third of the tomato sauce over the bottom of the lasagne | Lay a third of the spinach on top, followed by a third of the squash | Drizzle over a quarter of the béchamel sauce | Repeat twice more with layers of pasta, then tomato sauce, spinach, squash and béchamel | Top with a final layer of pasta, using broken pieces to fill any gaps (try to avoid overlaps) and cover with the remaining béchamel | Put a few rosemary sprigs on top to garnish

Cover the lasagne with foil and put in the oven on the lowest shelf | Bake for 50 minutes | Remove the foil and bake for a further 15 minutes, stand for 10 minutes | Serve with a green salad and a little balsamic glaze

SPIRAL TART

This dish will test your arrangement skills (plus your patience!), but it's worth it for the photo-worthy result. This healthy tart is full of freshly roasted veggies with an ever-so-slightly spicy tomato base. It's best to use a peeler to get the optimum thickness, and make sure the height of the veggie strips is consistent for a nice, even tart.

SERVES 4–6

320g ready-rolled dairy-free
    shortcrust pastry
flour, for dusting
80g passata
½–1 tsp chilli flakes
30g fresh basil
1 tbsp balsamic glaze
3 aubergines
4 large carrots
3 courgettes
2 tbsp olive oil
salt and black pepper

Preheat oven to 180°C | Clean work surface dusted liberally with flour | Rolling pin (or use a clean, dry wine bottle) | Large bowl filled with water | 20–22cm tart tin

Unravel the pastry and roll it out on the floured work surface until it's roughly 5mm thick | Drape it over the rolling pin and lift it into the tin | Gently press the pastry into the edges of the tin with your fingers to line the base and sides | Use a knife to cut off the excess at the top of the tin

Spoon the passata on to the base and spread it out evenly with the back of the spoon | Sprinkle over the chilli flakes | Pick the basil leaves from the bunch and arrange them in an even layer all over the base | Drizzle over the balsamic glaze and set aside

Trim the ends from the aubergines, carrots and courgettes and slice the aubergine in half lengthways | Use a vegetable peeler to slice each into thin ribbons and put them into the bowl filled with water to soak for about 3 minutes (this makes them more supple and easier to shape) | Remove and pat dry with kitchen paper

Take 1 ribbon of each of the vegetables and lay them on top of one another, first courgette, then carrot, then aubergine | Roll them up into a tight spiral to resemble a rose | Place the spiral in the middle of the tart | Start spiralling the ribbons tightly from the central rose all the way out to the edges, rotating from courgette, to carrot, to aubergine

Once the tart is completely full of vegetables, season with salt and pepper and drizzle with the oil | Put the tray in the preheated oven and bake for 40 minutes | Test and if you prefer softer vegetables, cover with foil and bake for further 15–20 minutes | Take the tin out of the oven and slide the tart out of the tin

Bring your work of art to the table so that everyone can take a photo, then carefully cut into slices with a VERY sharp knife

THE BIG BOSH! ROAST

Whether it's Christmas, Thanksgiving or just a normal Sunday, a roast dinner is the epitome of traditional food. We've based ours around a glorious centrepiece mushroom Wellington, one which is rich, full of texture and incredibly moreish, and goes great with any gravy. This meal should satisfy even the fussiest of dinner guests.

SERVES 4–6 WITH LEFTOVERS

1 x portion Rosemary & Thyme Roast Vegetables ingredients (see page 130)
1 x portion Mushroom Wellington ingredients (see page 128)
1 x portion Red Wine Gravy ingredients (see page 131)

Preheat oven to 200°C | Line 2 baking trays with parchment paper | 1 large empty saucepan with a lid | 1 large saucepan of boiling water on a high heat | Large deep baking tray | Shallow baking tray | Large deep frying pan | Food processor | Pastry brush, optional | Pastry cutters, optional

Start with the Rosemary & Thyme Roast Vegetables by peeling and boiling the potatoes and parsnips following the instructions on page 130, up to the point when they're on their trays and cooling to room temperature

Meanwhile, assemble the Mushroom Wellington following the instructions on page 128 | Once the Wellington is ready to go in the oven, set it aside while you get on with the roast vegetables

Finish preparing the roast vegetables and put the tray on the second shelf of the oven, leaving enough space for the Wellington to fit on the top shelf later | Set the timer for 20 minutes

Start preparing the vegetables for the Red Wine Gravy following the instructions on page 131

When the timer goes off, put the Wellington on the top shelf of the oven and take out the roast vegetables | Gently shake the tray and return it to the oven | Set a timer for 30 minutes

15 minutes before the timer goes off, finish making the Red Wine Gravy | Take the roast vegetables and Wellington out of the oven and transfer to serving dishes | Serve!

MUSHROOM WELLINGTON

SERVES 6

7 garlic cloves

5 sprigs fresh rosemary

6 sprigs fresh thyme

4 portobello mushrooms (about 160g)

1 tsp + 1 tbsp olive oil

1 tsp salt, plus a little extra

2 tsp black pepper, plus a little extra

1 large red onion

2 tsp light brown sugar

300g chestnut mushrooms

125ml white wine

200g vacuum-packed chestnuts

250g pecans

2 slices seeded bread (about 80g)

2 sheets ready-rolled dairy-free
  shortcrust pastry

4 tbsp plant-based milk

Preheat oven to 200°C | Line 2 baking trays with parchment paper | Large frying pan on a medium heat | Food processor | Pastry brush, optional | Pastry cutters, optional

Peel and mince 4 of the garlic cloves using a sharp knife | Remove the leaves from 4 rosemary and 4 thyme sprigs by running your thumb and forefinger from the top to the base of the stems (the leaves should easily come away), then finely chop

Lay the portobello mushrooms on one of the lined baking trays with the stems pointing up | Drizzle 1 teaspoon oil over the gills of each mushroom and sprinkle with a little salt and pepper | Divide the chopped rosemary, thyme and garlic between the mushrooms | Put the tray in the oven and cook for 15 minutes | Remove and set aside

Meanwhile, peel and finely chop the red onion | Add the tablespoon of oil to the frying pan | Add the red onion to the pan and sauté for 10 minutes, stirring regularly, until softened

While the onions are cooking, peel and finely chop the remaining 3 garlic cloves | Remove the leaves from the remaining rosemary and thyme sprigs and finely chop | Measure 1 teaspoon salt, 1 teaspoon of the pepper and the sugar into a small bowl | Add the garlic, rosemary, thyme, salt, pepper and sugar into the pan and stir everything round for 1 minute

Put the chestnut mushrooms into the food processor and whizz until very finely chopped | Tip them into the pan, increase the heat to high and cook until softened and all the liquid has evaporated, about 5–7 minutes

Pour the white wine into the pan and stir it around for about 3 minutes, or until almost all the liquid has cooked off | Tip the mixture into a large mixing bowl and leave to cool for 5 minutes

Put the chestnuts, pecans and bread into the food processor and whizz until they resemble breadcrumbs (you may need to do this in batches) | Add to the bowl with the onions | Using a wooden spoon, thoroughly stir everything together until you have a thick dough-like mixture

Lay 1 pastry sheet on the other lined baking tray | Spread half the chestnut mixture lengthways down the middle of the pastry sheet | Use your hands to mould it into a rectangle shape with a flat top, leaving at least a 3cm gap on all four sides | This shape will dictate the shape of the Wellington so make sure it's nice and straight and level on top

Place the 4 cooked portobello mushrooms neatly on top of the chestnut mixture, stems facing up, making sure the sides of the mushrooms don't hang off the edges | Layer the rest of the chestnut mixture over the top, encasing the mushrooms | Smooth and shape into a neat, long, rectangular mound

Using a pastry brush or your finger, brush a little of the plant-based milk around the exposed pastry edge | Lay the second pastry sheet over the mushroom filling and press it all down well, ensuring there are no air bubbles | Seal the edges by pushing down all the way round the filling with your fingers | Trim any excess pastry from the edges, making sure you leave a 1½cm crust around the base of the Wellington | Set the excess pastry aside for later | Use a fork to crimp all around the edges of the pastry to firmly seal the Wellington and to make it look nice

Roll out the excess pastry if necessary and use a pastry cutter to cut out shapes | Brush the Wellington lightly with the plant-based milk and decorate the top with the pastry shapes | Brush the shapes with the plant-based milk | Pierce some air vents in the top of the Wellington with a fork or sharp knife

Put the Wellington in the oven and bake it for 40 minutes, checking after 30 minutes (if it looks ready, remove it from the oven) | Use a bread knife to carefully cut the Wellington into slices and serve

ROSEMARY & THYME ROAST VEGETABLES

SERVES 4–6

1.2kg Maris Piper or other fluffy potatoes
5 medium carrots
5 medium parsnips
1 small butternut squash
   (about 600g)
1 garlic bulb + 5 cloves
1 tbsp salt, plus a little extra
125ml olive oil
16 sprigs fresh thyme
8 sprigs fresh rosemary

Preheat oven to 200°C | 1 large empty saucepan with a lid | 1 large saucepan of boiling water on a high heat | Large deep baking tray | Shallow baking tray

Peel the potatoes, carrots, parsnips and butternut squash

Cut the carrots and parsnips lengthways into halves or quarters and cut out any tough cores from the parsnips | De-seed the butternut squash then cut it into roughly the same size pieces as the carrots | Break the garlic bulb into cloves and lightly squash them with the side of the knife

Cut the potatoes into thirds or quarters and put them in one of the saucepans | Fill the pan with cold water, sprinkle in the tablespoon of salt (to make them extra fluffy) and put the pan on a high heat | Bring to the boil and then cook for 5–8 minutes

Meanwhile, put the parsnips into the other pan and boil for 5 minutes | Drain and transfer to the large, deep baking tray to cool down

Put the butternut squash and carrots into the shallow baking tray and toss in 3 tablespoons of the oil, half the thyme sprigs and half the rosemary | Sprinkle over salt to taste | Toss it all together and set aside

When they're done, drain the potatoes and tip them back into the pan | Put the lid on and shake the pan for 15 seconds to scuff the outsides of the potatoes, then tip them on to the baking tray next to the parsnips and let them cool down to room temperature

Nestle the remaining thyme and rosemary sprigs and the garlic cloves you squashed earlier in among the potatoes and parsnips | Pour over the remaining olive oil and toss gently to coat

Put the tray with the potatoes on the second shelf of the hot oven and the tray with the carrots underneath (leave enough space above the top shelf for the Wellington if you're making the full roast) and cook for 50–60 minutes | Toss the veg every 20 minutes to ensure they are evenly cooked on all sides | They should be golden and crispy on the outside when they're done | If you want to give them an extra crispy boost at the end, turn on the grill and place one tray at a time under it | Keep a close eye on it, they should crisp up within just a few minutes

RED WINE GRAVY

A good gravy is the jewel in the crown of a great roast dinner, and this is a really good gravy. Try it drizzled over a plate of hot chips for an indulgent Yorkshire classic.

SERVES 6

1 red onion
1 small carrot
1 celery stick
2 tbsp olive oil
3 garlic cloves
1 sprig fresh rosemary
2 sprigs fresh thyme
350ml red wine
1 litre vegetable stock
3 tbsp cornflour
6 tbsp room-temperature water
1 tbsp tomato purée
1 tsp yeast extract (e.g. Marmite)
1 tsp English mustard
1 tsp dark brown sugar
½ tsp salt
½ tsp black pepper

Deep frying pan with a lid on a medium heat

Peel and finely dice the red onion, carrot and celery, keeping them separate on the chopping board

Pour the olive oil into the hot pan | Add the diced onion and cook for 2 minutes | Peel and crush the garlic cloves into the pan and stir everything together | Cook for 2 minutes until you've released the aroma of the garlic

Add the diced carrot and celery and the rosemary and thyme sprigs | Stir everything together on the heat for about 7 minutes, until the vegetables are well softened | Pour in the red wine and cook until most of the liquid has evaporated

Pour the vegetable stock into the pan | Turn up the heat so that it's bubbling nicely, then reduce to a gentle simmer, put the lid on and cook for 10 minutes

Take the pan off the heat and strain the liquid into a bowl through a sieve so that you're left with a clear stock | Pour it back into the pan and put it back on the heat

Put the cornflour into a small glass | Add the water and mix together with a fork, stirring really well to ensure there are no lumps

Add the cornflour mixture to the pan and whisk continuously while the gravy bubbles away for 5 minutes, until you have a nice, thick consistency | Add the tomato purée, yeast extract, mustard, sugar, salt and pepper and stir until well mixed | Pour the gravy into a jug ready to serve

MINTED MUSHY PEAS

SERVES 4

Small saucepan of boiling water on a high heat

300g frozen peas
1 tbsp dairy-free butter
10 fresh mint leaves
½ lemon
½ tsp salt
½ tsp black pepper

Pour the peas into the boiling water and bring back to the boil | Cook for 3 minutes | While the peas are cooking, put the rest of the ingredients into a bowl and mix together with a fork | Drain the peas and add them to the other ingredients | Blend lightly with a stick blender while the peas are still hot, ensuring roughly half of them remain whole | Stir to mix in all the seasoning

TARTARE SAUCE

SERVES 4

1 small shallot
½ lemon
½ tsp and a pinch of salt
15g capers
20g pickled gherkins
5g fresh tarragon
5g fresh chives
5g fresh parsley
100g vegan mayonnaise

Peel and finely slice the shallot and put it into a bowl | Squeeze over the juice of the lemon, catching any pips in your other hand, and add the pinch of salt | Finely chop the capers, gherkins, tarragon, chives and parsley and add them to the bowl | Add the vegan mayo, the ½ teaspoon of salt and stir everything together

WORLD'S BEST PESTO LASAGNE

We've been cooking and refining this pesto lasagne dish for years. It's an absolute show-stopper: rich, flavoursome and healthy(ish). It'll take you a while to make since there are a few different parts to combine, but it's so worth it – see the photos overleaf. Use light olive oil for a light, delicious pesto.

see the photos overleaf

SERVES 8

2 aubergines
2 courgettes
2 yellow peppers
2 red peppers
1 tbsp olive oil
12 lasagne sheets
salt and black pepper

FOR THE TOMATO SAUCE
2 tbsp olive oil
1 red onion
3 garlic cloves
100g pitted black olives
50g capers
700ml passata

FOR THE BÉCHAMEL
150g cashew nuts
450ml unsweetened plant-based milk
50g dairy-free butter
25g plain flour
25g nutritional yeast
2 tsp onion powder
1 garlic clove
½ lemon
100ml water

FOR THE PESTO
70g pine nuts
60g fresh basil
15g nutritional yeast
2 garlic cloves
½ lemon
150ml light olive oil

Preheat oven to 180°C | 3 baking trays | Large saucepan on a medium heat | Small saucepan on a high heat | Medium saucepan on a medium heat | Liquidiser | 30 x 20cm lasagne dish

Trim the aubergines and courgettes and cut them diagonally into slices about 1cm thick | Cut the peppers in half and cut out the stems and seeds, then cut them in half again | Divide the chopped vegetables between two of the baking trays, drizzle with the oil and sprinkle over a good pinch of salt and pepper | Put the trays in the hot oven and roast for 20 minutes, then remove and set aside

Next, make the tomato sauce | Pour the oil into the large saucepan | Peel and finely chop the onion and add it to the pan | Cook for 5–10 minutes, until soft | Peel and crush the garlic cloves into the pan, cooking for a further 2 minutes | Drain and roughly chop the olives and add them to the pan along with the capers, passata and a good pinch of salt and pepper | Reduce the heat to medium-low and leave to simmer for 25–30 minutes, stirring occasionally

Meanwhile, put the cashews in the small saucepan and bring to the boil | Boil for 10 minutes

To make the béchamel sauce, warm the plant-based milk in the microwave | Put the dairy-free butter in the medium saucepan and stir with a wooden spoon until it melts, then turn the heat right down and gradually add the flour to the pan, stirring vigorously until you have a doughy paste | Gradually pour in the warm plant-based milk, stirring all the time until you have a thick, creamy sauce | Keep stirring until the sauce thickens to the consistency of custard | Add the nutritional yeast and the onion powder | Peel and crush the garlic clove and add it to the pan | Squeeze the lemon juice into the pan, catching any pips with your other hand

Drain the boiled cashews and rinse them with cold water to cool them down | Put them in the liquidiser along with the water | Whizz to a fine cream with no bits | Pour the béchamel sauce into the liquidiser and whizz together | Season with salt and pepper | Pour into a bowl and set aside | Clean out the liquidiser

To make the pesto, spread the pine nuts over the clean baking tray, put it in the oven and toast for 3 minutes | Put them in the liquidiser along with the basil and the nutritional yeast | Peel the garlic cloves and add them to the liquidiser | Squeeze in the lemon juice, catching any pips with your other hand | Pour in the olive oil | Blitz everything together until you've made a fine pesto | Taste and season with salt and pepper

Cover the bottom and sides of the lasagne dish with a thin layer of tomato sauce | Put a layer of lasagne sheets over the bottom, without overlapping them | Use broken up bits of lasagne to cover any gaps or corners

Spread a third of the remaining tomato sauce on to the lasagne sheets | Place a third of the baked veggies on top | Spread a third of the cashew béchamel on top, spreading it all the way to the edges of the dish | Drizzle a third of the pesto sauce on top | Repeat twice more, making layers of pasta, tomato sauce, veggies and cashew sauce and topping with a long, arty drizzle of pesto

Cover the dish with foil, put it in the oven and bake for 45 minutes | Remove the foil and bake for 10 more minutes | Take it out of the oven and leave it to stand for 10 minutes before serving

04

GREENS
& BOSH!
BOWLS

It's protein o'clock
Get real healthy with BOSH! Bowls
And amazing greens

TOMATO & POMEGRANATE SALAD

This dish is extremely colourful and tasty. The zingy fresh tomato contrasts with the sweet, juicy bursts of the pomegranate seeds and the explosion of flavour from the fresh herbs. This surprising flavour combination creates the perfect sharing side salad for an Italian pasta, or would serve as a super-healthy light meal or side for a BBQ.

SERVES 4–6

2 slices brown bread
4 tbsp olive oil
1 lemon
1 tsp brown sugar
4 drops Tabasco, optional
400g baby tomatoes
1 small red onion
handful fresh parsley
handful fresh mint
1 pomegranate or
    100g pomegranate seeds
50g pea shoots or other salad greens
salt and black pepper

Medium frying pan on a low heat

Cut the bread into 1cm cubes | Heat 1 tablespoon of the olive oil in the pan and sauté the bread cubes for 2–3 minutes, tossing regularly until they are browned on all sides | Tip on to a plate and set aside

Cut the lemon in half and squeeze the juice into a large bowl, catching any pips in your other hand | Stir in the remaining 3 tablespoons of oil and the brown sugar and season with the salt and pepper and Tabasco, if using | Taste and adjust the seasoning if necessary

Halve the tomatoes, peel and finely slice the red onion, pick the leaves from the parsley and mint and add them all to the bowl | Remove the seeds from the pomegranate by rolling it first to loosen the seeds, then scoring around the middle and prising the two halves apart | Hold the halves over the bowl and tap the bottom of each half firmly with a spoon to release the seeds | Add the salad greens and croutons, toss gently and serve to impressed guests

LEMON & CHILLI GRIDDLED GREENS

This artfully simple side goes with anything. The keys are not to add any oil until the asparagus are cooked and to get really black char lines for depth of flavour, so try not to move the veggies around in the pan. This is a fast and easy side that makes the asparagus wonderfully tasty.

SERVES 2–3

200g asparagus
1 fresh red chilli
2 tbsp olive oil
½ lemon
salt

Dry griddle pan on the highest heat

Bend the asparagus spears until they snap and throw the woody ends away | Lay them in the hot pan, across the grill lines | Leave for about 2–3 minutes for thin spears or up to 5 minutes for thick spears | Don't move them until they have developed deep black char lines, then flip them over and repeat on the other side

Meanwhile, rip the stem from the chilli, cut it in half lengthways and remove the seeds, if you prefer a milder flavour, and finely chop | Once the asparagus stems are charred on both sides, drizzle over the oil and scatter over the chopped chilli | Squeeze the lemon over the veggies, catching the pips in your other hand | Sprinkle over a pinch of salt, stir and cook for another 60–90 seconds | Take off the heat and serve immediately

ULTIMATE BBQ COLESLAW

This is an awesome coleslaw. It feels fresh and healthy, but is also drenched in naughty BBQ sauce, which makes it incredibly indulgent. Serve inside the Big BOSH! Burger (see page 119) or as a side at a BBQ.

(see page 119)

SERVES 6–8

1 large red cabbage (about 950g)
olive oil
200g BBQ sauce
1 onion
2 carrots
salt and black pepper

FOR THE DRESSING
3 limes, plus a little extra
200g vegan mayonnaise
1 tsp English mustard
½ tsp hot sauce, optional
2 tsp salt
1 tsp black pepper
good pinch of cayenne pepper

Preheat oven to 180°C | Roasting tin | Pastry brush

Cut the cabbage in half, cut out and discard the core, then chop into about 8 pieces. Tip into a roasting tin | Brush the cabbage all over with oil and cover with the BBQ sauce | Season with salt and pepper | Put the roasting tin in the hot oven and cook for about 45 minutes, removing when the cabbage is nice and blackened, but not burnt | Let it cool down for 10 minutes

Halve the limes for the dressing and squeeze the juice into a bowl, catching any pips in your other hand | Add the rest of the dressing ingredients and stir to a smooth, well-mixed consistency

Peel and finely slice the onion | Peel the carrots and slice them thinly using a vegetable peeler or sharp knife | When the cabbage is cool enough to handle, slice the pieces finely

Put all the veg in a serving bowl and pour over the dressing | Stir well, taste and add more salt, pepper or lime juice as desired

GUACAMOLE POTATO SALAD

This is a winning creation – it's creamy, rich and luscious with a lime twist. This is the perfect side for a BBQ and brings back memories of childhood potato salads, but with a remixed, delicious Mexican flavour. This is a go-to dish of ours and we promise it will not disappoint.

SERVES 4–6

1kg new potatoes
25g dairy-free butter
1 lime
3 avocados
2 tbsp olive oil
60ml unsweetened plant-based milk
2 tbsp vegan mayonnaise
2 tsp garlic powder
2 tsp salt, plus a little extra
1 tsp black pepper
250g cherry tomatoes
1 large fresh red chilli
½ red onion
40g fresh coriander

Large saucepan with a lid | Liquidiser

Cut the potatoes into quarters (or halves if they're small) and put them in the saucepan | Fill the pan with cold water and add a large pinch of salt | Turn the heat to high and bring to the boil, then reduce the heat to low and simmer for 8–10 minutes, until the potatoes are cooked through | Drain and tip back into the pan | Add the dairy-free butter and stir it through the potatoes so that they're well covered, then set aside

Halve the lime and squeeze the juice into the liquidiser | Halve and carefully stone the avocados by tapping the stone firmly with the heel of a knife so that it lodges in the pits, then twist and remove the stones | Scoop the avocado flesh into the liquidiser | Add the olive oil, plant-based milk, vegan mayonnaise, garlic powder, salt and pepper and whizz to a thick cream, adding a splash more plant-based milk if needed

Dice the cherry tomatoes | Rip the stem from the chilli, cut it in half lengthways and remove the seeds, if you prefer a milder flavour, then finely chop | Peel and finely chop the onion | Put the chopped vegetables into a large serving bowl and add the dressing and potatoes | Chop the coriander leaves and finely slice the stalks and sprinkle into the bowl | Stir everything together so that it's well mixed, then enjoy!

FALAFEL BOSH! BOWL

This zingy, zesty salad with contrasting earthy falafel flavours is the perfect reward for a gym visit or as an accompaniment to a BBQ. You can make it ahead and, since it's so healthy, you can really fill yourself up and still feel great. Feel free to sub out the falafel if you just want a quick and easy Greek salad.

SERVES 4–6

100g leafy salad leaves
1 lemon
small handful fresh coriander leaves
handful fresh mint, optional

FOR THE HUMMUS
½ lemon
1 x 400g tin chickpeas
3 tbsp aquafaba (water from
    chickpea tin)
1½ tbsp tahini
1½ tbsp olive oil
1 garlic clove
1 tsp salt

FOR THE FALAFEL
2 x 400g tins chickpeas
2 small red onions
3 garlic cloves
15g fresh coriander leaves
15g fresh flat-leaf parsley leaves
100g gram flour
1½ tbsp harissa paste
2 tsp salt
1 tsp ground cumin
½ tsp black pepper
½ lemon
olive oil, for frying

FOR THE GREEK SALAD
½ cucumber
800g mixed tomatoes
½ small red onion
75g pine nuts (or any nuts)
150g pitted black Kalamata olives
    (but any olives will do)
3 tbsp red wine vinegar
3 tbsp olive oil
1 tsp dried oregano
salt and black pepper

Food processor | Large frying pan | Small frying pan

First make the hummus | Cut the lemon in half and squeeze the juice into the food processor, catching the pips in your other hand | Add all the rest of the ingredients and blend to a smooth paste | Scrape into a bowl and set aside (there's no need to rinse the processor bowl)

Now make the falafel | Drain the chickpeas | Peel and finely chop the red onions and garlic | Finely chop the coriander and parsley | Put all the falafel ingredients except for the oil and lemon in the food processor | Squeeze the lemon juice into the processor, catching any pips in your other hand | Whizz to a thick paste

Using wet hands to stop the batter sticking, pick out small pieces of falafel batter between your finger and thumb and create little balls 2–3cm in width (about the size of a large marble) until you've used up all the batter

Put the large frying pan on a high heat and add the olive oil | Add the balls to the pan and cook for 2–3 minutes until golden all over, using a spatula to flip them halfway through (you may need to do this in batches)

To make the salad, trim and slice the cucumber, cut the tomatoes into wedges and peel and thinly slice the onion | Put the small frying pan on a medium heat and put the pine nuts into the dry pan to toast for a few minutes | Tip the chopped vegetables into a large bowl with the toasted pine nuts and olives | Pour over the red wine vinegar and olive oil, sprinkle over the oregano and season with salt and pepper | Mix it all together

Get out four to six big bowls and lay a few salad leaves into each one | Fill each bowl with big helpings of Greek salad, hummus and falafel | Cut the lemon in half and squeeze over some juice, catching any pips in your other hand before serving with a sprinkling of fresh coriander and mint, if using

BEETROOT, ONION & SWEET POTATO SALAD

We wanted a salad with Beetroot, Onion, Sweet potato and Herbs (B.O.S.H., get it?). We love beetroot and were keen to base a salad around it. This is incredibly tasty and can be made even more filling by using two sweet potatoes or sprinkling some more nuts on top for a protein boost.

SERVES 4

1 sweet potato (2 if you're hungry)
4 garlic cloves
60ml + 2 tbsp olive oil
300g cooked beetroot
1 small red onion
3 tbsp white wine vinegar
2 tsp hot sauce
150g fresh or frozen peas
100g baby leaf spinach
large handful fresh coriander leaves
large handful fresh mint leaves
2 medium avocados
handful mixed nuts
salt and black pepper

Preheat oven to 200°C | Baking tray

Peel the sweet potato and cut it into 1cm discs | Lay them on the baking tray along with 3 unpeeled garlic cloves | Pour over the 2 tablespoons of oil and sprinkle with salt and pepper | Put into the hot oven for 20 minutes until soft and charring slightly at the edges | Remove and set aside

Meanwhile, finely slice the beetroot and place it in a bowl | Peel and mince the onion | Peel the remaining garlic clove and finely slice half (use the other half for something else) | Add both to the beetroot | Pour over the white wine vinegar, the 60ml of oil and the hot sauce | Mix well and leave to infuse while the sweet potato bakes

Put the peas into a small microwave-safe bowl, cover with a splash of water and cook on full power for 4 minutes | Quickly drain and run under cold water to cool, then add to the large bowl | Add the spinach | Finely chop the coriander and mint leaves and add to the bowl | Gently toss everything together

Just before you're ready to eat, halve and carefully stone the avocados by tapping the stones firmly with the heel of a knife so that it lodges in the pits. Twist and remove the stones | Run a dessert spoon around the inside of the skin to scoop out the avocado halves, then slice finely, trying to keep the shape of the avocado halves

Divide the salad between serving plates | Put a neat line of sweet potato slices on each plate and add a small pile of avocado | Spoon the beetroot over the plate | Roughly chop the nuts and scatter them over and enjoy this delicious, healthy meal!

SATAY SWEET POTATO BOSH! BOWL

This powerful salad combines some of our favourite ingredients: satay sauce, hummus and sweet potato. It's gluten-free, healthy and delicious! Peanuts feature heavily in this staple and incredibly moreish satay sauce of ours. Filled with protein and healthy goodness, this dish will leave you satisfied for ages!

SERVES 2

1 large sweet potato (about 280g)
½ red onion
olive oil
1–2 tsp chilli flakes
2 garlic cloves
210g pre-cooked quinoa
   (home-made or shop-bought)
150g broccoli (about ½ medium head)
1 avocado
handful crushed nuts
160g Hummus (shop-bought
   or see page 199)
2 tbsp seeds, to serve
salt and black pepper

FOR THE DRESSING
2 limes
2cm piece fresh ginger
1 garlic clove
1 fresh red chilli
10g fresh coriander
3 heaped tbsp good-quality
   crunchy peanut butter
1 tbsp soy sauce

Preheat oven to 180°C | Liquidiser | Roasting tray

Cut the sweet potato into 2½cm chunks, keeping the skin | Cut the red onion half into quarters and place in the roasting tray with the sweet potato | Drizzle over some olive oil, sprinkle over the chilli flakes and season with a little salt and pepper | Crush the unpeeled garlic cloves by pressing down on them with the back of a knife and add to the roasting tray | Put the tray in the oven for 15 minutes

Heat the cooked quinoa in the microwave | Break the broccoli into bite-sized florets | Take the tray out of the oven and add the broccoli, mixing everything around with a wooden spoon | Put the roasting tray back in the oven and bake for a further 15 minutes, until the potatoes and broccoli are softened | Remove from the oven

Meanwhile, make the dressing | Zest the limes, cut them in half and squeeze the juice into the liquidiser, catching any pips in your other hand | Peel the ginger by scraping off the skin with a spoon and roughly chop | Peel the garlic | Rip the stem from the chilli, cut it in half lengthways and remove the seeds, if you prefer a milder dressing | Roughly chop the coriander | Add all the ingredients for the dressing to the liquidiser and whizz it all up | Test for consistency, adding spoonfuls of water until it's runny enough to pour over the salad

Halve and carefully stone the avocado by tapping the stone firmly with the heel of a knife so that it lodges in the pit, then twist and remove the stone | Run a dessert spoon around the inside of the skin to scoop out the avocado halves, then slice

Divide the quinoa between two serving bowls | Arrange the roasted vegetables and nuts on the top | Add a large dollop of hummus and the avocado slices to the bowls | Drizzle a little dressing over the top of each and serve the rest on the side before sprinkling with seeds to serve

SOUTHWEST BOSH! BOWL

This was inspired by our desire to create the deliciousness of a burrito without the tortilla. It's a great source of protein and contains all your essential amino acids, making it a perfect post-workout meal for spring or summer. Fiery, citrussy, sweet and fresh, it's an orchestra of healthy goodness. Plus, avocados – need we say more?

SERVES 2–4

Medium saucepan | Liquidiser

140g cooked basmati rice (shop-bought or Perfectly Boiled Rice, see page 207)
1 x 400g tin black beans
1 x 200g tin sweetcorn
2 large tomatoes
½ red pepper
½ small red onion
2 small avocados
1 lime
½ fresh green chilli
1 tbsp olive oil
150ml unsweetened plant-based milk
1 tsp maple syrup
½ tsp garlic powder
1 baby gem lettuce
50g fresh coriander
hot sauce, to serve
salt and black pepper

Tip the pre-cooked rice into a mixing bowl, fluff it with a fork and transfer to a serving bowl

Drain the black beans and sweetcorn and add them to the rice

Halve the tomatoes, cut out the seeds and finely dice | Trim any stem and seeds from the pepper and finely dice | Peel and finely dice the onions | Add the diced vegetables to the rice and fold together

Halve and carefully stone the avocados by tapping the stones firmly with the heel of a knife so that it lodges in the pits, then twist and remove the stones | Scoop the flesh into the liquidiser | Cut the lime in half and squeeze in most of the juice, catching any pips in your other hand | Rip the stem from the chilli, cut it in half lengthways and remove the seeds, if you prefer a milder flavour | Add the chilli, olive oil, plant-based milk, maple syrup and garlic powder to the liquidiser and whizz to a creamy sauce with a thick drizzling consistency, adding a splash more plant-based milk if necessary | Taste and adjust the seasoning as needed

Finely slice the lettuce | Chop the coriander leaves and finely chop the stalks | Add the lettuce and coriander to the rice | Pour over the avocado dressing and stir everything together | Check the seasoning and add salt, pepper or remaining lime juice to taste

Spoon into bowls to serve, drizzled with a little hot sauce

THE BEST-DRESSED BOSH! BOWL

The combination of balsamic, fennel and garlic here lends a unique flavour to the roasted veggies – it's one of the most delicious ways to eat loads of goodness in one go. The dressing would suit any vegetables, just keep timing in mind to ensure they're properly cooked. Great as a light lunch, starter or BBQ side.

SERVES 3–6

1 onion
4 garlic cloves
1 fresh red chilli
1 tbsp fennel seeds
4 tbsp olive oil
4 tbsp balsamic vinegar,
    plus extra for drizzling
1 tbsp maple syrup
3 tbsp tomato purée
250g pre-cooked puy lentils
350g butternut squash
1 fennel bulb
200g cherry tomatoes
1 yellow pepper
1 red pepper
1 courgette
1 avocado
100g baby leaf spinach or kale
10g fresh flat-leaf parsley leaves
salt and black pepper

Preheat oven to 180°C | Medium saucepan on a medium heat | Roasting tray

Peel the onion | Peel the garlic | Rip the stem from the chilli then cut it in half lengthways and remove the seeds if you prefer a milder flavour | Finely chop the onion, garlic, chilli and fennel seeds | Spoon into the saucepan and add the 4 tablespoons of olive oil, balsamic vinegar, maple syrup and tomato purée | Stir for 5 minutes then add the cooked lentils | Stir through, remove from the heat and set aside

Peel the squash, cut it in half and remove the seeds, then cut into 2cm chunks | Tip into a roasting tray, drizzle with a little olive oil, season and put the tin in the hot oven for 15 minutes, then remove

Meanwhile, trim the fennel bulb, remove the core and cut into 1cm wedges | Halve the tomatoes | Cut the peppers in half, cut out the stems and seeds | Trim the ends of the courgettes | Cut the pepper and courgettes into 1cm pieces | Add the fennel, courgettes, peppers and tomatoes to the roasting tray with the squash and drizzle over a little more oil | Return to the oven to cook for 15 minutes, until tender

While the vegetables are roasting, halve and carefully stone the avocado by tapping the stone firmly with the heel of a knife so that it lodges in the pit, then twist and remove the stone | Run a dessert spoon around the inside of the skin to scoop out the avocado halves and cut into chunks | Wash and lightly chop the spinach or kale and roughly chop the parsley leaves

Remove the roasted veggies from the oven and tip into a serving bowl with the avocado, spinach or kale, parsley and lentils | Stir and serve

THE BIG GREEN BOSH! BOWL

This delicious dish is perfect post-gym fuel. It looks like a lot of food, but you'll wolf down the healthy greens and delicious dressing. Double up the recipe for a week's worth of turbo-sized lunches. This clever recipe uses the rice water to steam the veggies, so it's easy to cook and there's less washing up.

SERVES 2

1 x mug brown rice (about 200g)
2 x mugs water (about 600ml)
100g Tenderstem broccoli
50g green beans
200g tinned mixed beans
   (or any bean, such as kidney beans)
1 fresh red chilli
1 lemon
50g baby leaf spinach
12 cherry tomatoes
75g cashew nuts
85g Hummus (shop-bought
   or see page 199)
handful fresh coriander leaves
sriracha or other hot sauce, to serve
salt

FOR THE DRESSING
1 garlic clove
2cm piece fresh ginger
1 tbsp olive oil
1 tsp sesame oil
1 tbsp soy sauce

Medium saucepan with a lid on a medium-high heat | Kettle boiled | Steaming basket or metal colander

Fill a mug with brown rice, pour it into a sieve and rinse with cold water for 30 seconds | Use the same mug to measure twice as much boiling water into the hot pan | Add a little salt | When the water is boiling, add the rice, put the lid on, stir and cook for 20 minutes

Meanwhile, trim the bottoms from the broccoli | Top and tail the green beans

Next, make the dressing | Peel and finely chop the garlic | Peel the ginger by scraping off the skin with a spoon, chop and put in a mug with the garlic | Pour over the olive oil, sesame oil and soy sauce and stir

After 20 minutes, take the lid off the rice and put a steaming basket or heatproof colander on top of the pan | Add the green beans and broccoli and pour over half the dressing | Put a big lid on top of the basket or colander and set the timer for 5 minutes, then check the veg and rice are done, if not, cook for a little longer | Once everything is cooked, turn off the heat and leave the lid off the pan

Strain half the tin of mixed beans (use the other half another time) | Rip the stem from the chilli, cut it in half lengthways and remove the seeds if you prefer a milder flavour, then finely slice | Strain the rice if necessary | Cut the lemon in half

To assemble, divide the spinach between the bowls, followed by the mixed beans, steamed veggies, rice and cherry tomatoes | Pile the cashews on top of the salad and spoon on a large dollop of hummus | Squeeze over the juice of the lemon, catching any pips in your other hand

Drizzle the rest of the dressing over the top and sprinkle over the coriander leaves and chilli | Finish by squeezing a tablespoon of sriracha or hot sauce over everything

MAKE YOUR OWN BOSH! BOWLS

BOSH! bowls are protein-filled bowls of deliciousness. They are typically filled with plant-based proteins, green veg and a grain of some kind. They're perfect for after the gym, or just for feeding your hungry belly during a busy day. You can quickly knock them together with whatever you have in the fridge, just ensure you cover each of these bases to ensure tastiness and healthiness!

1. **Choose your grain**
   Brown or white rice
   Couscous
   Quinoa
   Rice noodles
   Soba noodles
   Wholewheat noodles

2. **Add your protein:**
   Black beans
   Butter beans
   Kidney beans
   Lentils
   Pinto beans
   Seitan
   Tempeh
   Tofu

3. **Trim and finely slice the vegetables, then roast or steam them and add to the bowl**
   Asparagus
   Beetroot
   Broccoli
   Carrots
   Courgettes
   Green beans
   Mushrooms
   Onions
   Peppers
   Sweet potatoes

4. **Finely slice some raw veg and add straight to the bowl and stir everything together**
   Avocado
   Chilli peppers
   Cucumber
   Greens
   Kale
   Lettuce
   Peppers
   Spinach
   Spring onions
   Sweetcorn

5. **Chop the herbs, chuck into the bowl and mix through**
   Basil
   Chives
   Coriander
   Dill
   Mint
   Parsley
   Tarragon

6. **Roughly chop some nuts or seeds, or leave whole and add raw or toasted and scatter over the top**
   Blanched almonds
   Cashew nuts
   Chia seeds
   Flaxseeds/linseeds
   Hazelnuts
   Macadamia nuts
   Mixed nuts
   Peanuts
   Pecans
   Pine nuts
   Pumpkin seeds
   Sesame seeds
   Walnuts

7. **Choose your dressing and drizzle it over**
   Proper Spanish Aioli (see page 192)
   Balsamic vinegar
   Hummus (see page 199)
   Baba Ganoush (see page 193)
   Olive Tapenade (see page 192)
   Mango chutney
   Mustard
   Lemon juice
   Olive oil
   Rich Satay Sauce (see page 193)
   Soy or coconut yoghurt-based dressing
   Soy sauce

05

SMALL PLATES & SHARERS

Pimp out your mini-bites
With delicious sharing plates
For sides or tapas

CAULIFLOWER BUFFALO WINGS

These delicious wings taste naughty but are actually healthy, since they're baked. The spices are gorgeously deep and the panko breadcrumbs give a crunchy coating that contrasts nicely with the smooth cauliflower. It's the perfect starter or dish to share with friends. We promise, you'll love it.

SERVES 2–4

1 large head of cauliflower
150g plain flour
300ml plant-based milk
2 tsp garlic powder
1 tsp onion powder
1 tsp ground cumin
1 tsp paprika
½ tsp salt
¼ tsp black pepper
100g panko breadcrumbs
120g dairy-free butter
200g buffalo hot sauce

FOR THE RANCH SAUCE
150g cashew nuts
150ml plant-based milk
1 tbsp lemon juice
2 tsp garlic powder
¾ tsp salt
¼ tsp black pepper
handful fresh parsley
4 chives

Preheat oven to 180°C | Line 2 baking trays | Small saucepan of boiling water on a high heat | Food processor or liquidiser

Add the cashew nuts to the pan of boiling water and boil for 15 minutes, then strain and run under cold water to cool slightly

Meanwhile, break the cauliflower into florets and cut the stem into bite-sized pieces

Put the flour, plant-based milk, garlic powder, onion powder, cumin, paprika, salt and pepper into a bowl and whisk to a batter | Pour the panko breadcrumbs into another bowl and rub them between your thumb and fingers to break into slightly smaller breadcrumbs.

Tip the cauliflower into the batter and toss to coat | Transfer to the bowl of breadcrumbs, a few pieces at a time, and toss gently until well coated | Spread the cauliflower pieces over the lined baking trays and bake for 20 minutes

Meanwhile, melt the dairy-free butter in the microwave and stir in the hot sauce

After 20 minutes, remove the tray from the oven, pour over the hot sauce and carefully roll the cauliflower around until the pieces are fully coated | Put the tray back in the oven for 20–25 minutes, until a sharp knife glides into the thickest parts of the cauliflower and the outsides are really golden brown and crispy | Remove from the oven

While the cauliflower is cooking, put all the ingredients for the ranch sauce except for the herbs into the food processor or liquidiser and whizz for 1–2 minutes until smooth and creamy | Transfer to a serving bowl | Finely chop the parsley and chives and add most of them to the sauce, reserving a little for garnish

Serve the cauliflower wings while they're still hot on a serving plate, sprinkled with the remaining herbs and with the ranch dip on the side

SHIITAKE TERIYAKI DIPPERS

Once you've had your fill of these dippers, there won't be mush-room left in your belly for anything else (ahem)! They are crunchy and crispy, sweet and sticky, deliciously mushroomy inside and covered by a sumptuous sauce. A healthy bake with the luxurious feeling of a deep fry, this is great nibble-fodder.

SERVES 2

25ml soy sauce
130ml water
½ tsp ground ginger
½ tsp garlic powder
2½ tbsp brown sugar
1 tbsp cornflour
250g shiitake or wild mushrooms
150g panko breadcrumbs

FOR THE BATTER
200ml plant-based milk
115g plain flour
2 tsp garlic powder
2 tsp onion salt

Preheat oven to 200°C | Line 2 baking trays | Small saucepan on a medium heat

Put the soy sauce, 100ml of the water, the ground ginger, garlic powder and sugar into the hot pan and simmer gently until the sugar dissolves

Put the cornflour and remaining 30ml water into a glass and stir with a fork until there are no lumps | Add to the pan, turn up the heat and bring to the boil, stirring as you go | Reduce the heat and simmer for 2–3 minutes, stirring frequently, until the sauce is syrupy and viscous | Pour into a bowl and set aside

Put all the ingredients for the batter into a mixing bowl and stir to combine | Cut any large mushrooms in half and add all the mushrooms to the batter to coat thoroughly

Put the panko breadcrumbs into a large bowl

One by one, roll the battered mushrooms in the breadcrumbs and place them on the lined baking trays | Put the trays in the oven and bake for 18–20 minutes, until the mushrooms are golden brown and crispy | Remove from the oven, put them in a serving bowl and serve with the teriyaki sauce

POPCORN FALAFEL

We call these 'nom nom balls', and they are unacceptably good for a dippy dinner party. Crispy, crunchy and moreish, you may need to make double helpings (served with hummus, obviously). They are the best dipping food we have ever tasted, good as a snack, great in pitta, and an audacious way to enjoy a Middle Eastern staple!

SERVES 6–8

1 small red onion

3 garlic cloves

2 x 400g tins chickpeas

220g flour, plus a little extra

15g fresh coriander

15g fresh parsley

2 tsp harissa paste

1 tsp ground cumin

2 tsp salt

1 tsp pepper

1 lemon

180g panko breadcrumbs

240ml plant-based milk

250ml vegetable oil, for frying

2 x portions Classic Hummus
    (see page 199), to serve

Line a large bowl with a clean tea towel | Food processor | Large deep saucepan | Line a plate with kitchen paper

Peel the onion and the garlic | Drain and rinse the chickpeas and tip them into the tea-towel-lined bowl | Pat the chickpeas dry to remove as much moisture as possible

Put the onion, garlic and chickpeas into the food processor | Add 100g of the flour, the coriander, parsley, harissa, cumin, 1 teaspoon of the salt and ½ teaspoon of the pepper | Cut the lemon in half and squeeze in the juice, catching any pips with your other hand | Whizz to a thick paste that's not too sticky (if it seems too wet, add another tablespoon or two of flour)

With lightly floured hands, take teaspoons of the mixture at a time and roll them into 2cm balls about the size of large marbles

Put the panko breadcrumbs into a bowl | Put the remaining flour, the plant-based milk and the remaining salt and pepper into a bowl and stir them together until you have a thick, creamy batter | Dip 2 or 3 balls at a time into the batter, shake off any excess and transfer them to the bowl of breadcrumbs, rolling them around until they are completely coated | Repeat until all of the balls are coated

Pour the vegetable oil into the large deep saucepan so that it comes no more than two-thirds up the side of the pan | Place the pan on a medium heat | When a small piece of bread dropped into the pan turns golden brown after 60 seconds, you are ready to go

Fry the falafels in batches of 10 for 3–4 minutes, then turn them over and fry for a further 3 minutes, until deep golden brown and crisp | Remove from the pan with a slotted spoon and drain on the kitchen paper to remove the excess oil | Serve with hummus

BANGIN' VEGGIE KEBABS

These are delicious and very good for you! The marinades are super quick to put together; if you don't have a blender or liquidiser, chop and mix in a big bowl until you get the right consistency. This is a great one for making in advance, since the marinades and veggies can be stored in the fridge. These go so well with a dipping sauce, and are perfect for a quick meal or BBQ. See them in their glory on the next page.

MAKES 8

2 red, orange, green or yellow peppers
1 red onion
1 courgette
1 aubergine
150g cherry tomatoes
250g mushrooms
1 x portion Rich Satay, Spicy Shashlik or
    Asian BBQ marinade (see opposite)

Preheat oven to 180°C | Blender or liquidiser | Small baking tray | Wooden skewers, soaked

Cut the peppers in half and cut out the stem and seeds | Peel the onion | Trim the courgette and aubergine | Cut all the vegetables into 2.5cm chunks, put them in a big bowl and cover them with your chosen marinade | Stir everything together until it's really well mixed

Thread the marinated vegetables onto the wooden skewers, leaving 3cm free at either end | Lay the skewers across the baking tray, resting each end on the edges so that the vegetables are suspended above the base (as if they're being spit-roasted)

Put the tray in the hot oven and roast for 20–25 minutes, until the vegetables are cooked through, deeply caramelised and slightly crispy on the outside

MARINADES

Blender or liquidiser

Prepare your ingredients and then put them all into the blender or
liquidiser | Whizz to a smooth paste

ASIAN BBQ

MAKES 200ML

2 fresh red chillies, stemmed
6 garlic cloves, peeled
2½cm piece fresh ginger, peeled
10g fresh coriander leaves
½ tsp black pepper
4 tbsp agave syrup
2 tbsp white wine vinegar
2 tbsp soy sauce

SPICY SHASHLIK

MAKES 320G

2 large red chillies, stemmed
2 green bird's eye chillies, stemmed
6 garlic cloves, peeled
5cm piece fresh ginger, peeled
2 tbsp sunflower oil
2 tsp ground cumin
1 tsp ground coriander
1 tsp garam masala
½ tsp ground turmeric
2 tsp smoked paprika
½ tsp chilli powder
small handful fresh coriander
2 tbsp tamarind paste
2 tbsp cornflour
4 tbsp white wine vinegar
4 tbsp plain soy yoghurt
1 tsp sea salt
¼ tsp black pepper

RICH SATAY

MAKES 250G

juice of 2 limes
1 fresh red chilli, stemmed
1 garlic clove, peeled
2cm piece fresh ginger, peeled
10g fresh coriander
150g good-quality crunchy
    peanut butter
1 tbsp soy sauce
1–2 tbsp water, optional, to
    achieve runny consistency

SPICY SHASHLIK

RICH SATAY

HOI SIN PANCAKES

Everyone's favourite Chinese sharer – rich, salty mushrooms combine with the fresh green veggies and sweet hoi sin sauce to create a starter that no one can refuse. This is delicious with Asian dishes like our Crispy Chilli Tofu (see page 46) or Sticky Shiitake Mushrooms (see page 30). You can also replace the pancakes with gem lettuce leaves and simply wrap them into little healthy parcels.

SERVES 2 AS A STARTER

2 tsp vegetable oil
300g mushrooms (portobello, if possible)
2 tbsp soy sauce
1 tsp five-spice powder
1 tbsp rice vinegar
2 tsp sesame oil
1 tsp sugar
½ cucumber
3 spring onions
5 tbsp hoi sin sauce
8 Chinese pancakes

Small frying pan on a medium heat

Put the oil into the pan | Roughly slice the mushrooms, add them to the pan and cook for 10 minutes until their juices have cooked off | Add the soy sauce, five-spice, rice vinegar, sesame oil and sugar | Continue to cook, stirring continously until any additional sauce has mostly evaporated and the mushrooms are beautifully cooked and glazed

Meanwhile, halve the cucumber and remove the watery core with a spoon, then finely slice into 6cm matchsticks | Trim the top and bottom of the spring onions and cut them into matchsticks | Put the cucumber and onions on to a small plate and pour the hoi sin sauce into a small dish

Heat the pancakes following the instructions on the packet

When the mushrooms are ready, transfer them to a plate and serve them alongside their accompaniments | To assemble the pancakes, simply take a little of each ingredient and wrap them up into delicious pancake rolls

FRENCH ONION SOUP

A French classic presented in near-classic form. This is one for those long winter nights when you need something soothing and warming, great as a starter or served with chunky bread (perhaps spread with our Garlic & Herb Cashew Cheese on page 210) as a hearty meal for two. Be patient with the onions and you'll be rewarded with incredible flavour.

SERVES 2–4

50g dried porcini mushrooms
700ml boiling water
3 tbsp olive oil
6 large onions (about 750g)
6 garlic cloves
1 tsp brown sugar
2 tbsp dry sherry or port
½ tsp balsamic vinegar
½ lemon
½ tsp sea salt
¼ tsp black pepper
chunky bread, to serve, optional

Kettle boiled | Large saucepan on a medium heat

Put the mushrooms in a small bowl and cover with the boiling water

Pour the oil into the pan | Peel and finely slice the onions and add them to the pan | Peel and finely chop the garlic and add to the pan with 2 tablespoons of water | Stir everything together, reduce the heat to low, cover and cook very gently for 40 minutes, stirring every couple of minutes, until the onions turn a deep caramel colour | Add a tablespoon of water every now and again to prevent the onions from sticking | After 40 minutes, add the sugar and stir

Strain the liquid from the mushrooms into a bowl, squeezing out as much liquid as possible (keep the mushrooms for making a risotto or something else) | Pour the liquid from the mushrooms over the onions, add the sherry and balsamic vinegar, stir everything together and bring to a boil | Immediately reduce the heat to low and simmer gently for 10 minutes

Squeeze in the juice from the lemon, catching any pips in your other hand | Season with salt and pepper, spoon into bowls and serve on its own or with chunky bread, if using, to mop up the soup

SPANISH TAPAS

Look no further for a Mediterranean feast! Any or all of these dishes would be great accompaniments to Pettigrew's Paella (see page 114), served alongside Proper Spanish Aioli (see page 192), Olive Tapenade (see page 192) and a small bowl of olives. Or why not try them as party canapes (if you can get past the garlic flavours!). And they would match perfectly with red wine.

JANE'S PAN CON TOMATE

Imagine an effortlessly simple Spanish bruschetta that's ready in minutes yet feels exotic. This one is a favourite of Henry's mum, Jane, and her well-honed Spanish palate.

MAKES 8 SLICES

3 tomatoes
3 garlic cloves
small handful fresh parsley
60ml olive oil
2 tbsp white wine vinegar or
    sherry vinegar
sugar, to season, optional
8 slices good-quality bread
salt and black pepper

Toaster or grill | Coarse grater

Grate the tomatoes into a bowl | Peel the garlic and finely chop along with the parsley, then add to the bowl | Add the olive oil and vinegar and stir everything well | Taste and add salt, pepper and even a little bit of sugar, if using, to taste

Slice the bread into 2cm thick slices and toast until lightly browned | Spread the tomato dressing all over the toast with a knife or the back of a spoon, rubbing the mixture into the bread, and serve

PERI PERI HASSELBACK POTATOES

Halfway between a baked potato and a French fry, this quirky way to serve potatoes looks impressive but is simple to prepare. This goes great with a Big BOSH! Burger (see page 119) or as a side for a BBQ.

SERVES 4

4 large white potatoes
4 tbsp olive oil, plus extra for drizzling
6 tbsp dairy-free yoghurt
paprika, to sprinkle
garlic powder, to sprinkle
1 tbsp hot sauce
1 tbsp chopped chives, to serve
sea salt

FOR THE PERI PERI SPICE RUB
1½ tsp paprika
1½ tsp onion powder
1 tsp garlic powder
1 tsp dried oregano
1 tsp ground ginger
½ tsp cayenne pepper
½ tsp salt

Preheat oven to 180°C

Place one of the potatoes on a chopping board and lay a wooden spoon on either side (these will provide a stopping point so that you don't cut all the way through your potatoes) | Take a sharp knife and carefully cut very thin slices all the way along the potato, stopping when the knife hits the spoon handles | Repeat until all the potatoes have been 'hasselbacked'

Cut 4 rectangles of foil large enough to cover each potato | Put one potato in the centre of each and pull the sides up to form little nests | Drizzle 1 tablespoon olive oil over each potato, making sure the oil gets in between all the slices

Measure the spices for the spice rub into a small bowl and stir to combine | Use a teaspoon to sprinkle equal amounts of the spice rub over, and in between the slices, of each potato | Wrap the potatoes up in the foil ensuring there are no gaps | Place on a baking tray, put the tray in the oven and bake the potatoes for 45 minutes | Take the baking tray out of the oven and set it down on a heatproof mat | Turn the oven up to 220°C

Carefully open the parcels and flatten down the foil around the potatoes, being careful not to burn your fingers | Use the tip of a knife to lightly prise open the slices | Drizzle a touch more olive oil and sprinkle a little more salt over the potatoes | Put the tray back in the oven with the foil nests unwrapped and bake for a further 20–30 minutes

Spoon dairy-free yoghurt into a small dish and sprinkle with paprika and garlic powder | Spoon some hot sauce on top and swirl it through the yoghurt | Take the potatoes out of the oven | Lift them out of the foil nests and transfer to plates | Spoon the spice oil that's gathered in the foil nests over the potatoes | Garnish with chopped chives and serve with the spiced dairy-free yoghurt

ALL THE SAUCES

Oh dips, how we love you. These quick-to-make, guaranteed-to-please dips add another level of flavour to any meal in this book and impress any of your dinner guests. They're perfect party fodder: try serving a selection with fries, bread and sides for a buffet to rule them all. Or they are all delicious served with salads, pizzas, fries, crisps, crudités, you name it! See the whole selection in their rainbow of colours on page 196.

OLIVE TAPENADE

MAKES 300G

Food processor or stick blender

200g black olives, such as Kalamata, preferably pitted
2 garlic cloves
3 tbsp capers
10g fresh parsley, optional
½ lemon
5 tbsp olive oil

Remove the stones from the olives if they are not already pitted | Peel and crush the garlic into the food processor (or into a bowl if you're using a stick blender), and add the olives, capers and parsley, if using | Squeeze in the juice from the lemon, catching any pips in your other hand | Whizz to a rough purée

Pour in the olive oil bit by bit and give it a couple more pulses until very well combined, but still retaining some texture | Transfer to a serving bowl

PROPER SPANISH AIOLI

MAKES 75ML

Pestle and mortar (or use a small bowl and a wooden spoon)

5 garlic cloves
1 tsp sea salt
½ lemon
115ml olive oil

Peel and thinly slice the garlic and put it in the mortar (or bowl) with the sea salt | Squeeze in the lemon juice, catching any pips with your other hand | Bash to a fine pulp using the pestle (or wooden spoon) | Add a teaspoon of the oil and mash thoroughly into the garlic pulp, ensuring it is well mixed in | Repeat until all the oil is used up, making sure you only add a teaspoon of oil at a time and that each time the oil is fully incorporated before continuing, otherwise the mixture will split

RICH SATAY SAUCE

MAKES 250G

2 limes
1 fresh red chilli
1 garlic clove
2cm piece fresh ginger
150g good-quality crunchy
    peanut butter
10g fresh coriander
1 tbsp soy sauce

Food processor or stick blender

Finely zest the limes, then cut them in half and squeeze out the juice, catching any pips in your other hand | Rip the stem from the chilli into the food processor or bowl and remove the seeds, if you prefer a milder sauce | Peel the garlic | Peel the ginger by scraping off the skin with a spoon

Add all the ingredients to the food processor or a bowl and blend until smooth | Test the consistency, adding 1–2 tablespoons water to get the sauce as runny as you like | Taste and season with more lime juice or soy sauce if necessary

BABA GANOUSH

MAKES 300G

2 medium aubergines (about 500g)
2 small garlic cloves
1 lemon
2 tbsp tahini
3 tbsp olive oil
1 tsp cumin seeds
½ tsp smoked paprika
½ tsp salt
any combination of fresh chopped
    parsley, chilli flakes and/or harissa
    paste, to serve, optional

Preheat oven to 240°C | Line a baking tray | Food processor or stick blender

Pierce the skin of the aubergines a few times with a fork | Put onto the lined baking tray and place on the highest shelf in the oven | Cook for 20–25 minutes, turning once or twice, until the skin is blackened all over | Remove to a bowl and leave to cool

Meanwhile, peel the garlic and put it in the food processor (or a bowl) | Cut the lemon in half and squeeze in the juice, catching any pips in your other hand | Add the tahini, olive oil, cumin, paprika and salt

Cut the aubergine in half and use a large spoon to scoop out the flesh (or peel off the charred skin with your fingers) | Transfer the aubergine flesh to the food processor (or bowl) along with a few pieces of the charred skin to add flavour | Whizz until smooth

Taste and add a little more lemon juice or salt, if needed | Garnish with a few toppings, if using, such as the chopped parsley leaves, chilli flakes and/or harissa

RICH
SATAY SAUCE

AMAZING
CHILLI SAUCE

OLIVE TAPENADE

BANGIN' SALSA

ULTIMATE
GUACAMOLE

FIERY
CHILLI PESTO

BABA GANOUSH

PROPER
SPANISH AIOLI

ALL THE HUMMUS

Simple, tasty and universally loved, the wonderful hummus is a must in any discerning cook's repertoire. We like to freestyle with ours and create different flavours, each one a slightly remixed version of the original. So rather than give you one dish, here are eight ideas for how you could pay your own respects to the granddaddy of dips, the lifelong partner of falafel. Check out the photos overleaf to see the mouthwatering options.

Hummus is effortless to make – 5 minutes with a blender and you are done. Our classic recipe is used in our Mezze Cake (see page 98), Middle East Pizza (see page 108) and would go well with pretty much any dish in this book.

ROASTED GARLIC HUMMUS

MAKES 300G

1 large garlic bulb (5–10 cloves)
1 x 400g tin chickpeas
1 tbsp tahini
1 tsp salt
2 tbsp lemon juice
2 tbsp olive oil
2 tbsp water
15g fresh chives

Preheat oven to 160°C
| Food processor

Put the garlic bulb on a baking tray, put the tray in the oven and roast for 30 minutes | Remove and leave to cool, then peel | Drain the chickpeas | Put the roasted garlic, chickpeas, tahini, salt, lemon juice, oil and water into the food processor and whizz to a smooth paste | Finely chop the chives and stir them through at the end

SUN-DRIED TOMATO HUMMUS

MAKES 300G

1 x 400g tin chickpeas
1 garlic clove
5 sun-dried tomatoes
½ tsp dried oregano
¼ tsp sea salt
2 tbsp lemon juice
1 tbsp sun-dried tomato oil from the jar

Food processor

Drain the chickpeas | Peel the garlic | Put all the ingredients into the food processor | Whizz to a smooth paste and serve

OLIVE TAPENADE HUMMUS

MAKES 300G

1 x 400g tin chickpeas
1 garlic clove
50g pitted Kalamata olives
1 roasted red pepper from a jar
15g fresh parsley leaves
¼ tsp sea salt
2 tbsp lemon juice
2 tbsp olive oil

Food processor

Drain the chickpeas | Peel the garlic | Put all the ingredients into the food processor | Whizz to a smooth paste and serve

BURRITO HUMMUS

MAKES 300G

1 x 400g tin black beans
10g fresh coriander leaves
1 tsp ground cumin
½ tsp salt
¼ tsp black pepper
2 tbsp lime juice
2 tsp chipotle sauce

Food processor

Drain the black beans | Put all the ingredients into the food processor | Whizz to a smooth paste and serve

CLASSIC HUMMUS

MAKES 300G

1 x 400g tin chickpeas
2 small garlic cloves
2 tbsp tahini
¾ tsp salt
4 tbsp water
2½ tbsp lemon juice
2 tbsp olive oil

Food processor

Drain the chickpeas | Peel the garlic | Put all the ingredients into the food processor | Whizz to a smooth paste and serve

PESTO HUMMUS

MAKES 300G

1 x 400g tin chickpeas
1 garlic clove
20g fresh basil leaves
2 tbsp tahini
1 tbsp nutritional yeast
½ tsp salt
3 tbsp water
2½ tbsp lemon juice
2 tbsp olive oil

Food processor

Drain the chickpeas | Peel the garlic | Put all the ingredients into the food processor | Whizz to a smooth paste and serve

GUACUMMUS

MAKES 300G

1 avocado
200g tinned chickpeas
15g fresh coriander leaves
¾ tsp salt
½ tsp chilli flakes
2 tbsp lime juice
2 tbsp olive oil
2 tbsp water

Food processor

Drain the chickpeas | Halve and carefully stone the avocado by tapping the stones firmly with the heel of a knife so that it lodges in the pits, then twist and remove the stones | Scoop the flesh into the into the food processor and add the rest of the ingredients | Whizz to a smooth paste and serve

SATAY HUMMUS

MAKES 300G

1 x 400g tin chickpeas
3 tbsp smooth peanut butter
1 tsp smoked paprika
1 tsp chilli flakes
¼ tsp sea salt
2 tbsp unsweetened plant-based milk
2 tbsp water
1 tbsp olive oil
1 tbsp lime juice
1 tsp soy sauce

Food processor

Drain the chickpeas | Put all the ingredients into the food processor | Whizz to a smooth paste and serve

PESTO HUMMUS

CLASSIC HUMMUS

ROASTED
GARLIC HUMMUS

SUN-DRIED
TOMATO HUMMUS

OLIVE TAPENADE
HUMMUS

GUACUMMUS

SATAY HUMMUS

BURRITO HUMMUS

FLUFFY NAAN BREAD & RAITA

Indian meals are such fun and for us it's so much more satisfying to have a fluffy naan bread to complement your core curries. These breads and accompanying raita dip are quick to prepare and will ensure a home-cooked feast that transcends any takeaway. The naans are easy enough, just give them a bit of time to rise. Trust us, it's worth it.

BASIC NAAN BREAD

MAKES 4 LARGE NAAN BREADS

FOR THE BASIC NAAN DOUGH
1 x 7g sachet dried yeast
220ml warm water
2 tbsp sugar
6 tbsp plant-based milk
2 tsp salt
400g strong white bread flour,
    plus extra for dusting
vegetable oil

Large mixing bowl | Stand mixer fitted with the dough hook, or dust a clean work surface liberally with flour | Large frying pan | Rolling pin or a clean, dry wine bottle | Pastry brush

Put the yeast and warm water into the mixing bowl and stir to combine Set aside for 10–15 minutes until the mixture has started to froth

Once the yeast has activated, add the sugar, plant-based milk, salt and flour | Stir with a wooden spoon and bring it together to form a soft and sticky dough | Transfer the dough to the stand mixer, if using, and knead for 6 minutes, otherwise tip it on to the floured work surface, dust your hands with more flour and knead for 10–12 minutes by pushing the back half of the dough away with the heel of one hand, folding it back over the dough, giving it a quarter turn and repeating

Clean and dry the mixing bowl and grease the inside with a little vegetable oil | Place the dough in the bowl, cover it loosely with cling film or a plastic bag and leave it in a warm spot for 60–90 minutes, or until it's doubled in size

Once the dough has doubled in size, knock out the air by punching it in the bowl and then knead for another 1–2 minutes | Dust the work surface with at least 6 tablespoons of flour | Turn out the dough and coat it in the flour so that it's no longer sticky | Roll the dough into a ball and use a sharp knife to divide it in half and then half again, so that you have 4 equal balls of dough weighing about 170g each | Roll each ball in flour again to prevent sticking

Dust the rolling pin or wine bottle with more flour and roll out the balls of dough to form rough teardrop shapes

Pour 1 tablespoon vegetable oil into the large frying pan and place it on a medium heat

One by one, fry the naans for 5 minutes, turning them over halfway through, until golden and slightly charred on both sides (if they puff up during cooking, flatten them down firmly with a spatula to ensure they cook through) | Remove the naans from the pan

GARLIC NAAN BREAD

The classic. Garlicky and a little oily, this is so moreish it will guarantee you are full after your meal. You'll also feel like a master chef creating a naan from scratch.

MAKES 4 LARGE NAAN BREADS

1 x portion Basic Naan dough
(see page 203)
60ml olive oil
5 garlic cloves
small handful fresh coriander leaves,
to serve
salt

Large mixing bowl | Stand mixer fitted with the dough hook, or dust a clean work surface liberally with flour | Small saucepan | Large frying pan | Rolling pin or a clean, dry wine bottle | Pastry brush

Make the naan dough following the instructions for Basic Naan Bread (see page 203)

While the dough is rising, pour the 60ml olive oil into the small saucepan | Peel and crush the garlic cloves into the pan | Put the pan on a medium heat and cook the garlic until it turns just slightly golden, about 1–2 minutes (it will cook a bit more once it's off the hob, so make sure you don't overcook it) | Sprinkle over a small pinch of salt and set aside

Fry the naans for 5 minutes, turning them over halfway through, until golden and slightly charred on both sides (if they puff up during cooking, flatten them down firmly with a spatula to ensure they cook through) | Remove them from the pan and, while they're still hot, liberally brush each naan on both sides with the garlic oil | Scatter over some fresh coriander leaves and serve immediately

JANE'S MINT RAITA

Henry's mum taught him this incredibly simple dish at a young age. It's basically just yoghurt, mint and veg, but the addition of lemon gives it a real zing. Feel free to experiment with different veg combinations; it can be made with fresh mint, but we find the tart mint sauce contrasts well with the sugar.

SERVES 2–4

200g plant-based yoghurt
½ onion
½ tomato, or about 6 cherry tomatoes
¼ cucumber
½ tsp sugar
½ tsp salt
2 tsp mint sauce
pinch of cayenne pepper, plus a little
extra to serve
½ lemon

Put the plant-based yoghurt into a bowl | Peel and finely chop the onion and add it to the bowl | Finely chop the tomato and cucumber and add them to the bowl with the sugar, salt, mint sauce and cayenne pepper | Squeeze in the juice of the lemon, catching any pips in your other hand | Taste and adjust the seasoning if necessary | Sprinkle over a little more cayenne pepper to serve for a splash of colour

PESHWARI NAAN BREAD

Peshwari naans are so sweet and delicious it's almost like eating a dessert. But a good one improves any savoury dish it's eaten with, the little crumbly bits of coconut falling out adding an extra topping to your curry. They are surprisingly easy to make – and totally worth it.

MAKES 4 LARGE NAAN BREADS

1 x portion Basic Naan dough
  (see page 203)
80g blanched almonds
30g raisins
2 tbsp caster sugar
30g desiccated coconut
3 tbsp vegetable oil

Large mixing bowl | Stand mixer fitted with the dough hook, or dust a clean work surface liberally with flour | Liquidiser | Rolling pin or a clean, dry wine bottle | Large frying pan

Make the naan dough following the instructions for Basic Naan Bread (see page 203), up to where the dough is divided into 4 pieces

Put the almonds, raisins, caster sugar and desiccated coconut into the liquidiser and whizz for 1–2 minutes, until you have a coarse mixture

Flour the rolling pin or wine bottle and roll out one ball of dough to a rough circle | Place a quarter of the filling mixture into the centre of the circle | Dust your hands with flour, lift up the edges of the dough with your fingers and pinch them together in the centre so that the filling is fully enclosed | Gently flatten the filled dough ball and roll it out into a rough teardrop shape | Repeat with the remaining balls of dough

Pour the vegetable oil into the large frying pan and place it on a medium heat | One by one, fry the naans for 5 minutes, turning them over halfway through, until golden and slightly charred on both sides (if they puff up during cooking, flatten them down firmly with a spatula to ensure they cook through) | Remove the naans from the pan and serve immediately

SPECIAL
FRIED RICE

PERFECTLY
BOILED RICE

ONION
FRIED RICE

RICE 3 WAYS

Humans have been thriving on rice for centuries. Here we'll show you an awesome way to cook it, taught to Henry by his father, that will ensure your rice is perfect every time. And what's even better than rice? Fried rice, obviously. We love it as a speedy dish to enjoy on its own or to jazz up any meal. You can also speed things up by using pre-cooked rice, which is available in most supermarkets.

PERFECTLY BOILED RICE

This is a really neat way to ensure perfect rice every time. You could add a knob of peeled ginger, a slice of lemon or a jasmine teabag for flavoured rice. It's super simple. Just remember: double the quantity of water to rice, lid on, lowest heat, 12 minutes, BOSH! Works every time.

SERVES 1–2

½ mug basmati rice (about 100g)
1 mug water (about 300ml)
salt

Medium pan with a tight-fitting lid on a high heat | Kettle boiled

Rinse the rice under cold running water | Drain and transfer to the pan | Add the mug of freshly boiled water and a large pinch of salt | Put the lid on and bring to the boil | Give one stir with a spoon and immediately reduce the heat to the lowest setting | Put the lid back on and cook for 12 minutes | Don't touch the rice until the time is up

After the timer has gone off, take the pan off the heat

ONION FRIED RICE

This wonderful rice will add a little extra to any Indian curry. It's quick, simple, but delicious. Try alongside our Rogan BOSH! (see page 74), Creamy Korma (see page 71) and Garlic Naan (see page 204).

SERVES 1–2

1 small red onion
6cm piece fresh ginger
2 tbsp vegetable oil
1 tbsp cumin seeds
2 tbsp soy sauce
½ tsp chilli flakes, optional
1 x portion Perfectly Boiled Rice
    (see page 207) or 1 x packet
    pre-cooked basmati rice

Large frying pan on a medium heat

Peel and thinly slice the onion | Peel the ginger by scraping off the skin with a spoon and finely grate

Add the oil to the frying pan | Add the cumin seeds and fry for about 1 minute until they are a shade darker and aromatic | Add the grated ginger and fry for another minute

Add the red onion and continue to fry for 5–6 minutes, until the onion is softened | Add the soy sauce, chilli flakes, if using, and the cooked rice | Combine everything together and serve immediately

SPECIAL FRIED RICE

This gorgeous fried rice is good enough to eat on its own, but would also work perfectly with any Thai or Chinese main course. It's also great for a quick feed when you get home after a late night!

SERVES 1–2

80g firm tofu
3 garlic cloves
2 spring onions
1 small carrot
1 small red pepper
1½ tbsp vegetable oil
1 tbsp toasted sesame oil
50g garden peas
50g sweetcorn
1 tsp ground turmeric
1 tsp curry powder
½ tsp black pepper
1 tbsp brown sugar
1 tbsp dairy-free butter
1 x portion Perfectly Boiled Rice
    (see page 207) or 1 x packet
    pre-cooked basmati rice
3 tbsp soy sauce
handful fresh coriander, to serve
salt

Tofu press or 2 clean tea towels and a weight such as a heavy book | Saucepan | Wok or large frying pan on a high heat

Press the tofu using a tofu press or place it between two clean tea towels, lay it on a plate and put a weight on top | Leave for at least half an hour to drain any liquid and firm up before you start cooking

Peel and finely chop the garlic | Trim the roots of the spring onions, roughly chop the green parts and finely chop the white stems | Peel the carrot and chop it into 5mm cubes | Cut the pepper in half and cut out the stem and seeds, then slice into 5mm cubes

Pour the oils into the wok or frying pan | Add the carrot, red pepper, garlic and spring onions, leaving aside some of the green parts to scatter over later | Stir-fry for 1 minute

Crumble in rough pieces of the tofu | Add the peas, sweetcorn, turmeric, curry powder, pepper and sugar | Stir-fry for another 6–8 minutes, until the vegetables are cooked through | Add the dairy-free butter, rice and soy sauce and stir everything together | Season with salt to taste

Garnish with the coriander leaves and the remaining chopped spring onions and serve immediately

GARLIC & HERB CASHEW CHEESE

It's amazing how easy it is to make delicious, healthy cream cheese from mostly store-cupboard ingredients. If we need a quick cheese to go in a pasta or on toast, this is our go-to recipe. Cashews are the magic ingredient here and you'll need a badboy blender to get the cheese nice and smooth.

MAKES 400G

310g cashew nuts
60ml water
1 tsp salt
2 tbsp coconut oil
1 tbsp nutritional yeast
1 lemon
1 garlic clove
small handful fresh parsley leaves
6–8 chives

Medium saucepan of water on a high heat | Food processor or liquidiser

Put the cashew nuts in the pan of hot water and boil for 15 minutes until they are soft and have rehydrated (alternatively, you can soak them overnight in cold water) | Drain the nuts and tip them into a food processor or liquidiser with 30ml fresh water | Whizz for 60 seconds until you have a thick, smooth, creamy paste with no bits

Add the remaining 30ml water, the salt, coconut oil and nutritional yeast (you want a thick, gloopy consistency so add more water if necessary) | Cut the lemon in half and squeeze in the juice, catching any pips in your other hand | Peel the garlic and add it to the food processor or liquidiser | Whizz for a few minutes until the mixture is very smooth, scraping down the sides with a spatula every now and then to make sure everything is mixed

Transfer the completely smooth mixture to a bowl | Finely chop the parsley and chives and stir them through the mixture with a spoon

Lay out a large piece of cling film on a clean work surface and spoon the mixture into the middle | Fold over the cling film and roll up the cheese into a log, squeezing out any air and tightening the ends of the cling film as you go | Refrigerate for at least 2 hours to set fully

06

COCKTAILS

When you're in the mood
Reach for the cocktail shaker
And wow with these drinks

EASY ALMOND BAILEYS

You can make this quick version of Baileys in less than five minutes. It was inspired by our favourite bartenders, Susie and Tim, and it's the drink to cosy up in front of a movie with. Make a big batch and leave it in the fridge for up to a week, just give it a good shake before serving.

MAKES 500ML

400ml unsweetened almond milk
60ml Jack Daniels
50ml freshly brewed espresso
3 tbsp agave syrup or maple syrup
1 tsp vanilla essence
ice, to serve, optional

Large jug | Shot measure | Tumblers

Measure all the ingredients into a large jug and stir with a fork until mixed | Serve neat in tumblers over ice, if using

SALTED CARAMEL ESPRESSO MARTINI

This is a fantastic way to feel both sophisticated and a little bit excited. Just whack some caffeine in your drink to add instant liveliness to your evening. Espresso martinis are a go-to in the BOSH! household. Just make sure to be responsible – one or two of these beauties is plenty! Everyone who tries this goes 'mmm' and a photo is guaranteed.

MAKES 2

8–10 ice cubes
25ml coffee liqueur (like Kahlùa)
50ml vodka
50ml espresso
10ml caramel syrup
½ tsp salt
6 coffee beans, to serve

2 martini glasses | Cocktail shaker

Put some ice in your empty martini glasses to cool them down | Fill the cocktail shaker with ice

Put the coffee liqueur, vodka, espresso, caramel syrup and salt into the cocktail shaker, put the lid on and shake vigorously to mix

Pour into the chilled glasses, decorate with the coffee beans and serve

If you're gonna be drinking, why not give yourself the gift of some nutrients at the same time? That's the inspiration behind our 'Smoochies' – hooch smoothies. Why not create your own Smoochie bar at your next party and let your guests make their own? We call this pre-hab – getting your good deeds done in advance (of a boozy night, that is). Drink a few of these and you'll be merry but also glowing and full of antioxidants, vitamins and goodness. You may still have a hangover, so don't drink too many!

MANGO
HARD

WATERMELON
HEAVEN

GINGER
NINJA

FRUITY
FIRE

WATERMELON HEAVEN

This is deliciously daiquiri-like, but filled with fruit and flavour
and just a touch of merry rum.

MAKES 4 MARTINI GLASSES

1 mango (about 240g)
150g strawberries
1 lime
175g frozen watermelon chunks
40g green grapes
1 slice fresh pineapple (about 100g)
2 ice cubes, plus a little extra
125ml spiced rum (5 shots)
fresh watermelon slices, to serve

Liquidiser | 4 martini glasses | Paper straws, optional

Peel the mango and cut as much flesh from the stone as you can | Remove the stalks from the strawberries

Cut the lime in half and squeeze the juice into the liquidiser, catching any pips in your other hand, then add all the fruit and the ice cubes | Pour in the rum | Whizz it all up until it's like a thick, cold slushy | Add more ice if you need to make it thicker

Serve in martini glasses with slices of fresh watermelon on the side and paper straws, if using

GINGER NINJA

Ginger, carrots, orange and vodka – that's gotta be healthy,
right? It's also delicious. This really is a guilt-free party!

MAKES 4 GLASSES

2½cm piece fresh ginger
300g carrots (3 medium)
1 orange
150ml water
2 tbsp maple or agave syrup
150ml vodka
½ lime
ice, to serve

Liquidiser | 4 highball glasses

Peel the ginger by scraping off the skin with a spoon | Trim the carrots | Peel the orange and remove the pith

Put the ginger, carrots, orange, water, syrup and vodka into the liquidiser | Squeeze in the lime juice, catching any pips in your other hand, and whizz until completely smooth

Fill the glasses with ice, pour over the drink, and enjoy!

FRUITY FIRE

Fresh watermelon is a delicious, feel-good ingredient guaranteed to make you feel healthy and happy all at the same time. Add strawberries, banana, pineapple and lime and you are in for a win! This is ready-made summer in a glass, and full of natural goodness.

MAKES 4 GLASSES

Liquidiser | 4 highball glasses

120g fresh strawberries, plus 4 to serve
½ ripe banana (about 50g)
100g fresh pineapple
240g fresh watermelon
   (without the rind)
1 lime
½ orange
150–200ml spiced rum
ice, to serve

Remove the stalks from the strawberries and peel the banana | Cut the skin off the pineapple and trim the top and bottom, then cut into chunks | Add all the fruit to the liquidiser, squeezing in the lime and orange juice, catching any pips in your other hand | Whizz until smooth | Add 150ml of the rum, and add more to taste

Put some ice in your serving glasses | Pour in the boozy smoothie and garnish with a strawberry wedged on to the side of each glass

MANGO HARD

We are big rum fans and the combination of mango, banana and spiced rum is simply delicious. It'll transport you away to a beach in the South Pacific, if only for a moment. And the goodness in all the fruit has gotta be good in your body, right?

MAKES 4 GLASSES

Liquidiser | 4 highball glasses

½ apple (about 90g)
1 orange (about 120g peeled weight)
½ banana (about 50g)
½ mango (about 120g)
1 cup (about 130g) ice cubes,
   plus extra to serve
125–150ml spiced rum
1 lime, to serve

Peel and core the apple | Peel the orange and remove the pith | Peel the banana | Peel the mango and cut as much flesh as you can from the stone | Add all the fruit except the lime to the liquidiser with the ice cubes and the spiced rum and whizz until smooth | Cut the lime into slices

Serve the smoochie with ice and the slices of fresh lime

MIAMI VICE

Henry discovered this cocktail on a trip to the Bahamas and the flavours will take you straight there. It's an unbelievably tasty mix of strawberry daiquiri and piña colada – the perfect summer cocktail – and it's super impressive to behold. Get it really thick as it will melt as you drink it – you'll need a straw for this one!

MAKES 2 X 500ML GLASSES

Small saucepan on a medium heat | Liquidiser | Jug | 2 x 500ml glasses | Straws (we recommend paper straws – they're better for the planet!)

FOR SIMPLE SYRUP (WITH LEFTOVERS)
250ml water
200g caster sugar

FOR THE STRAWBERRY DAIQUIRI
250g strawberries
15ml grenadine
60ml white rum
12–24 ice cubes

FOR THE PIÑA COLADA
45ml coconut cream
45ml pineapple juice
pineapple slice, optional
60ml white rum
12–24 ice cubes
2 strawberries, to decorate

To make a simple syrup, put the water and sugar into the saucepan and warm through for about 5 minutes, stirring continuously until all the sugar has dissolved | Remove from the heat and leave to cool | Keep any syrup you don't use in the fridge for another time

Next make the strawberry daiquiri | Remove the stems from the strawberries and put the fruits into the liquidiser with the grenadine, white rum and 45ml of the simple syrup you made earlier | Add 12 ice cubes and blend to a beautiful purée | If it's not so thick that it hardly moves, add more ice, you are looking for a thick, snow-like consistency | Once it's a very thick, smooth purée, pour it into a jug | Rinse out the liquidiser

Now make the piña colada | Put the coconut cream, pineapple juice, 45ml simple syrup, pineapple slice, if using, and white rum into the liquidiser | Add 12 ice cubes and blend, aiming for a thick, stiff-peak consistency as before | Add more ice if you need to

Put a large wooden or metal serving spoon in the middle of one of the glasses | Pour both cocktail mixtures into the glass at the same time, one on either side of the spoon (you may need a friend to help you with this) | Pour all the way to the top, leaving a nice icy bump way above the top of the glass | Remove the spoon | Repeat with the second glass | Top your cocktails with fresh strawberries, pop in straws and enjoy your culinary trip to the Bahamas!

MOJITOS

Rum. Lime. Mint. Spice. A quartet of wins makes these mojitos amazing. Perfect on a summer's day, they are fresh, crispy and sweet, but with exotic, spicy flavours that are perfect with Asian dishes. Mojitos are usually made with a muddler to squash the lime, but the bottom of a rolling pin or a spoon will work just fine.

SPICY MOJITO

MAKES 4

4 limes

24 fresh mint leaves, plus 4 sprigs
    to serve

8 tsp caster sugar

2 tsp Tabasco sauce

4 handfuls ice

200ml white rum

200ml soda water

4 fresh bird's eye chillies

4 highball glasses | Muddler or rolling pin

Cut the limes into wedges and divide them between the glasses | Muddle (squash) them into the bottom of the glass to release the juices (be careful not to break the glass if it's thin)

Divide the mint leaves and the sugar between the glasses | Add the Tabasco sauce (use a little or a lot, this really depends on your palate) | Lightly crush everything together with the muddler to make sure the flavours are well mixed

Fill the glasses with ice | Pour the rum between them and stir everything together until the sugar has dissolved | Pick the leaves from the sprigs of mint

Put a little soda water into the glasses as a topper, garnish with fresh mint leaves, add a chilli to each glass and serve

GINGER & LEMONGRASS MOJITO

MAKES 4

3 limes

24 fresh mint leaves, plus 4 sprigs
    to serve

4 handfuls ice

200ml white rum

500ml soda water

4 sprigs fresh mint

FOR THE FLAVOURED SYRUP

5cm piece fresh ginger

8cm lemongrass stalk

1 lime

6 tbsp sugar

6 tbsp water

Small saucepan | 4 highball glasses | Muddler or rolling pin

First make the flavoured syrup | Peel the ginger by scraping off the skin with a spoon and grate it into the saucepan | Trim the root of the lemongrass, peel away the tough outer layers and chop into small pieces, then add to the pan | Cut the lime in half and squeeze in the juice, catching any pips in your other hand | Add the sugar and water and stir everything together

Put the pan on a medium heat for about 5 minutes, stirring all the time so the sugar dissolves | Take off the heat and set aside to cool to room temperature | Strain into a jug through a sieve

Cut the 3 limes into wedges and divide them between the glasses along with the mint leaves | Squash into the bottom of the glass with a muddler or the end of rolling pin to release the juices (be careful not to break the glass if it's thin)

Put a handful of ice into each glass and pour a measure of rum and a measure of syrup into each one | Stir everything together | Add a splash of soda water into each glass and garnish with sprigs of fresh mint

WATERMELON JÄGERBOMB PUNCH

We came up with this at the end of the first ever BOSH! shoot. We had a watermelon, a Galia melon, energy drink and a bottle of Jägermeister. We put the video live and it had 20 million views within a week! Use a really big watermelon and give the outside of the Galia melon a really good scrub before you put it inside.

SERVES 8

1 very large watermelon (at least 50cm diameter)
1 Galia melon (that will comfortably fit inside your watermelon)
2 x 250ml cans energy drink
8–12 ice cubes
handful fresh strawberries or blueberries
350ml Jägermeister

Liquidiser or stick blender

Choose which side will be the bottom of the watermelon; if it doesn't stand up straight, use a knife to slice a very small sliver off the base | Once it's standing upright, cut horizontally across the middle | Take off the top and keep it for another recipe

Scoop out all the watermelon flesh and seeds from the bottom half until the inside looks neat | Transfer the flesh to the liquidiser and blend (or use a stick blender and a bowl), then pour into a large bowl through a sieve to remove any seeds

Scrub the Galia melon with a brush to make sure it's clean | Lay it on its side and slice off the top 4cm | Scoop out the seeds and discard | Scoop out the melon flesh and transfer it to the liquidiser | Whizz and then pour through a sieve into the bowl with the watermelon juice | Save the melon shell, this will act as your shot glass

Pour the energy drinks into the melon juice and stir | Now pour half the juice mixture into the hollowed-out watermelon | Carefully place the hollowed-out Galia melon into the middle of the watermelon so that it's floating in the melon juice

Drop ice cubes and berries into the melon juice around the edges | Pour the Jägermeister into the Galia melon (don't fill it too much in case it sinks) | Top up the edges with more melon juice to fill the watermelon bowl (you might have some left over, which you can use to refill later on)

Take the watermelon to the party, lift out the Galia 'shot glass' and drop it back into the watermelon punch bowl in front of all your guests so that the Jägermeister spills into the melon juice | Wait for the applause

07

DESSERTS

Please your mouth with these
Scrumptious desserts and puddings
To make your friends smile

SHIRLEY'S SHEFFIELD SCONES

Ian's mum, Shirley, always makes him a batch of these wonderful scones when he's back home. They are really tasty, easy and incredibly addictive. The cashew clotted cream is amazing, and combined with the crumbly scones and sweet jam gives a flavour and texture sensation. Be careful not to overbake them, you're looking for a very light colour.

MAKES 8

240g self-raising flour
40g caster sugar
½ tsp salt
40g dairy-free butter
120ml plant-based milk
50g sultanas
raspberry jam, to serve

FOR THE CASHEW CREAM
140g cashew nuts
1½ tbsp icing sugar

Preheat oven to 200°C | Line a baking sheet | Small saucepan of boiling water | Food processor | Liquidiser or hand beater | Cooling rack

To make the cashew cream, put the cashews into the boiling water and cook for 15 minutes | Take off the heat, strain and run under cold water to cool slightly | Put them into the liquidiser with the icing sugar and a splash of water and whizz to a thick cream (or use a hand beater), adding more water if the mixture is too thick

Meanwhile, put the flour, caster sugar, salt, dairy-free butter and plant-based milk into the food processor and whizz to a dough | Take the blade out, tip in the sultanas and fold them into the mixture

Pull out roughly golf-ball-sized pieces of dough (about 3cm each) and roll them into balls between your palms | Place on the lined baking sheet and squash until they're roughly 1cm thick, leaving a little space between each one as they will expand in the oven | Put the baking sheet in the oven and bake for roughly 12 minutes, until lightly golden | Remove and transfer to the cooling rack to cool

Serve the scones with a thin spread of dairy-free butter, a good dollop of raspberry jam and the cashew clotted cream

CHOCOLATE CHIP COOKIES

These are the perfect cookies – crunchy on the outside and gooey on the inside. Plus, they're incredibly easy to make and even easier if you use a food processor. Best served warm (of course), you could also add nuts, raisins or dried fruit but, as self-confessed minimalists, we are perfectly happy with just the melted chocolate chips.

MAKES 25

250g dairy-free butter
225g caster sugar
2 tsp vanilla extract
1 tbsp golden syrup
300g plain flour
1 tsp baking powder
½ tsp salt
85g dark chocolate

Preheat oven to 180°C | Line 2 baking sheets with parchment paper | Food processor, optional | Wire rack

Put the dairy-free butter, sugar, vanilla extract and golden syrup into the food processor and whizz to a cream | Pour in the flour, baking powder and salt and whizz everything together (you could also do all this in a big bowl with a wooden spoon) | Turn off the food processor and remove the blade | Chop the dark chocolate into small chips and fold them through the mixture with a spatula until they're evenly spread

Spoon walnut-sized pieces of the mixture on to the lined baking sheets, leaving 5cm between each ball of dough (you may need to cook them in batches) | Squash the balls to flatten them slightly (but not flat like pancakes)

Put the baking sheets in the oven and bake for 12–14 minutes, swapping them over halfway through so that they cook evenly | When they are ready the cookies should be golden around the edge, but paler in the middle | Take the baking sheets out of the oven but leave the cookies on them for 5–10 minutes to firm up a little, then transfer carefully to wire racks to cool

SPANISH BEACH CHURROS

We remember eating churros on the beach in Spain as kids and decided we needed to recreate the memory (even if we are in East London in the rain!). This is such an easy dish to make, you could even make a giant churros snake if you were feeling adventurous. Trust us, try this, you will thank us!

MAKES 12−15

215g sugar

2 tsp ground cinnamon

1½ litres + 2 tbsp vegetable oil (preferably flavourless, like sunflower)

500ml water

½ tsp salt

½ tsp vanilla extract

240g plain flour

FOR THE CHOCOLATE SAUCE

100g dark chocolate

185ml plant-based milk

40g sugar

½ tsp vanilla extract

Small saucepan on a low heat | 3 disposable piping bags or 1 clean reusable piping bag | 1½cm star-shaped nozzle | Large deep saucepan | Cooking thermometer, optional | Baking tray lined with parchment paper | Medium saucepan | Line a large plate with a double layer of kitchen paper

First, make the chocolate sauce | Break up the chocolate and put it into the small saucepan with the plant-based milk, sugar and vanilla | Stir to a smooth sauce | Transfer to a serving bowl | Set aside

Sprinkle 115g sugar and the cinnamon over a large plate and set aside

If you are using disposable piping bags, pile them up and roll them together to make one thick cone (a single bag is likely to split) | Cut a small hole at the tip, insert the piping nozzle and push it all the way down to the bottom so that it sticks out of the hole | Spray or brush the inside of the bag with a little oil | If you are using a reusable bag, insert the nozzle and coat lightly with oil

Pour the 1½ litres of oil into the large saucepan so that it comes a third of the way up the sides of the pan | Heat the oil to about 180°C, or until a wooden spoon dipped into the oil sizzles around the edges

Meanwhile, put the water, the remaining 100g sugar, the 2 tablespoons vegetable oil, salt and vanilla extract into the medium saucepan and place on a high heat | Bring to the boil, stirring to dissolve the sugar | Remove from the heat, add the flour and beat vigorously with a wooden spoon until it forms a thick, sticky dough (you'll need to use a little elbow grease) | Spoon the mixture into the piping bag

Pipe 6 churros on to the lined baking tray, each one about 10−15cm long | Carefully transfer the churros to the hot oil (if you're feeling brave you can pipe them straight into the oil) | Fry for 8−10 minutes, until golden and cooked through | Use a wooden spoon to move them around if they stick together

Remove the churros with a slotted spoon and lay on the kitchen paper for 1 minute to drain | While they're still hot, transfer to the cinnamon sugar and roll until completely covered | Repeat with the remaining dough − you may need 3 or 4 batches | Serve with chocolate sauce

GOOEY PBJ BROWNIES

A surprising combination of two American classics – brownies and peanut butter jelly (aka jam). The tart, sweet jam contrasts with the earthy peanut and complements the sticky chocolate. Be careful not to overcook the outside – under is better than overdone with this one. For extra power-up points, serve with vegan ice cream and top with melted dark chocolate and nuts.

SERVES 12

300g plain flour
460g light muscovado sugar
160g cocoa powder
1 tsp baking powder
½ tsp salt
120g smooth peanut butter
   (thinner is better for this)
220ml water
220ml vegetable oil
2½ tbsp vanilla extract
50g dark chocolate
120g raspberry jam
80g raspberries
2 tbsp broken peanuts

Preheat oven to 160°C | 20 x 30cm cake tin | Parchment paper | Food processor or electric beater

Line the cake tin with the parchment paper, making sure there's a good overhang (this excess will act as handles to remove the brownie from the tin when it comes out of the oven)

Add the flour, sugar, cocoa, baking powder and salt to the food processor and whizz to combine | Add 30g of the peanut butter, the water, oil and vanilla | Blend until everything is well mixed (or put everything in a large mixing bowl and use an electric beater) | Break the dark chocolate into squares and add it to the mixture | Blend for another few seconds to mix in the chocolate

Use a spatula or metal spoon to empty the brownie mix into the cake tin and smooth it out so it goes all the way to the edges of the tin | Use a spoon to pour and drag swirls of the remaining peanut butter and the jam randomly over the top of the brownie, decorating the whole top with long swirls of jam | Push the raspberries and peanuts randomly into the mix

Put the tin in the hot oven and bake for 45 minutes, until cooked but still squidgy in the middle (try to avoid the outsides drying out and getting too brown, you want to take it out sooner than you think – the middle will still be soft and maybe even wobbly, but it will cool down to a gooey perfection)

Take the tin out of the oven and let it cool down almost to room temperature | Use the parchment paper to lift the brownie out of the tin and put it on a chopping board (you may need a friend to help with this to ensure it doesn't break in the middle) | Cut into brownie portions and serve

CARROT CAKE

Carrot cake is a favourite for many, and moist (what a word!) describes this version perfectly. It's sweet, wholesome and as succulent a cake as you'll ever have tasted, with the perfect spice combination of cinnamon, nutmeg and ginger and sweet, creamy icing. Decorate with walnuts to add the final bit of sizzle.

SERVES 8

4 medium carrots (about 380g)
2 tbsp flaxseeds
6 tbsp warm water
250g plain flour
300g brown sugar
1½ tsp baking powder
1½ tsp bicarbonate of soda
2 tsp ground cinnamon
2 tsp ground nutmeg
1 tsp ground ginger
2 tsp vanilla extract
120ml vegetable oil
1 tbsp apple cider vinegar
¼ tsp salt
120ml plant-based milk
75g sultanas
50g walnut halves
zest of 1 lemon

FOR THE ICING

80g dairy-free butter at room
    temperature, plus extra for greasing
3 tsp vanilla extract
450g icing sugar
½ lemon

Preheat oven to 180°C | 18cm deep, loose-bottomed cake tin | Parchment paper | Food processor or electric beater

Lay the base of the cake tin on the parchment paper and draw a circle around it, cut it out | Grease the inside of the tin with dairy-free butter, lay the paper circle in the bottom and then grease some more

Trim and finely grate the carrots | Put the flaxseeds into a small bowl, add the warm water and stir them around until you have a smooth paste | Leave for 5 minutes to thicken

Put the flour, sugar, baking powder, bicarbonate of soda, cinnamon, nutmeg and ginger into the food processor | Add the vanilla extract, vegetable oil, apple cider vinegar, salt and plant-based milk, along with the flaxseed paste | Whizz to a batter (or beat everything together in a large mixing bowl with an electric beater for 2–3 minutes)

Pour the batter into a mixing bowl | Add the sultanas and the grated carrot and fold everything together | Pour the batter into the tin and put the tin in the oven | Bake for 50–55 minutes, until a skewer inserted into the centre of the cake comes out clean | Take the cake out of the oven and let it cool to room temperature

Meanwhile, clean the food processor or electric beater | Now make the icing | Put the dairy-free butter, vanilla extract and icing sugar into the food processor or a clean bowl | Squeeze the lemon juice into the bowl, catching any pips in your other hand | Whizz to a thick cream that is thick but spreadable

Cut the cake in half horizontally and spread a third of the frosting over the base | Sandwich with the top half and spread the rest of the frosting over the top of the cake | Decorate with the walnut halves and lemon zest | The cake will keep in the fridge for up to 3 days

PAIN AU CHOCOLAT LOAF CAKE

This is the most ridiculous thing we could think to do with ready-bake dairy-free chocolate croissants. It's silly, zany, fun and tasty, and watching the croissants rise in the oven makes you feel like a kid again. Be sure to skewer them so they stay nice and straight while they bake.

SERVES 8

FOR THE CAKE

6 ready-bake dairy-free pains
    au chocolat (e.g. Jus-Rol)
200g plain flour
200g caster sugar
3 tbsp cocoa powder
2 tsp bicarbonate of soda
½ tsp salt
5 tbsp vegetable oil
1½ tsp vanilla extract
1½ tsp distilled white vinegar
125ml water
125ml plant-based milk

FOR THE ICING

100g icing sugar
75g cocoa powder
30g dairy-free butter, plus a little
    extra for greasing
40ml plant-based milk
½ tsp vanilla extract

Preheat oven to 160°C | 900g loaf tin | Parchment paper | Long wooden skewer | Food processor or electric hand beater

Line the loaf tin by cutting a strip of parchment paper that is a little longer and wider than the base of the tin, so you can use the parchment to pull out the cake when it's ready | Grease the inside of the tin with a little dairy-free butter

Prepare the pains au chocolat following the instructions on the packet | Line them up down the middle of the loaf tin, standing them on their ends | Rest the skewer on top of the tin, following the line of pastries and resting the tips on either end | Carefully twist the skewer into and through the top of the first pain au chocolat to attach it | Repeat with all the pastries until they're attached to the skewer | The skewer gives the pastries stability and keeps them standing upright

Put all the rest of the ingredients for the cake into the food processor and whizz to a batter (or put into a mixing bowl and beat together for 2–3 minutes with an electric hand beater)

Pour the cake mixture evenly down each side of the tin (it should fill the tin to about three-quarters full) | Cover the tin with foil and put it in the hot oven | Bake for 30 minutes, then remove the foil, put it back in the oven and bake for a further 20–25 minutes, until the cake is firm and a skewer inserted into the middle comes out clean (this additional cooking will give the pains au chocolat a lovely crispy top) | Remove from the oven and leave to cool in the tin | Clean out the food processor

Once the cake has cooled to room temperature, lift it out of the tin with the parchment paper and lay it on a serving plate | Remove the skewer

Put all the icing ingredients into the clean food processor and whizz to a thick, rich icing | Carefully spread the icing over the cake part of the loaf (don't spread it on the pains au chocolat) | Leave to firm up and serve

ULTIMATE CHOCOLATE FUDGE CAKE

Inspired by our most popular video ever, this is arguably the greatest chocolate cake we've ever tasted. Easy to make and delicious to eat, it's perfect birthday-cake fodder. Just make sure you have a gym membership, as this one is super indulgent. How naughty? Very naughty. Go on. Do it.

SERVES 8

120g plain flour
150g cocoa powder
1½ tbsp baking powder
1 tsp vanilla extract
250ml maple syrup
350ml plant-based milk
dairy-free butter, for greasing

FOR THE CHOCOLATE ICING
150g cocoa powder
200g icing sugar
60g dairy-free butter
1 tsp vanilla extract
65ml plant-based milk

Preheat oven to 180°C | 2 x 20cm cake tins | Parchment paper | Food processor or electric beater | Cooling rack | Spatula or long smooth knife

Lay the cake tins on the parchment paper and draw circles around the bases, then cut out the circles | Grease the inside of the tins with dairy-free butter and lay the paper circles in the bottom | Grease with more dairy-free butter

First make the cake | Put the flour, cocoa powder, baking powder, vanilla extract, maple syrup and plant-based milk into the food processor and whizz to a batter (or put in a bowl and whisk with the electric beater for 1–2 minutes)

Pour half the cake batter into each tin, making sure it is divided equally | Put the tins in the oven on the middle shelf and bake for 25 minutes | Don't worry if the tops of the cakes crack a little while baking, this will all be covered in icing later | Wash the food processor

Take the cakes out of the oven and let them cool to room temperature in the tins | The sponges will be quite fragile, so carefully turn them out of the tins on to the cooling rack and put the rack in the refrigerator for at least 30 minutes (this will make the icing process easier)

To make the icing, put the cocoa powder, icing sugar, dairy-free butter, vanilla extract and plant-based milk into the food processor and whizz to a really thick, smooth icing (or put them in a bowl and whisk with the electric beater)

Take one layer of the cake and put it on a large plate | Cover the top with a third of the chocolate icing | Lay the second cake on top | Cover the whole cake with the rest of the icing | Put the cake in the fridge for 1 hour to firm up | Remove the cake from the fridge, cut it into slices and serve

AQUAFABA CHOCOLATE MOUSSE

This is effortlessly simple and yet one of the most delicious chocolate mousses we've ever tasted. Decadent and luxurious, it's made with a handful of ingredients and can be prepared in advance and left in the fridge for later. The magical thrill of the aquafaba transformation (and the ensuing conversations with your guests!) is really something.

SERVES 3

100g dark chocolate
liquid from 1 x 400g tin chickpeas
    (aquafaba, about 130ml)
2½ tbsp sugar
1 tsp vanilla extract
pinch of salt
handful blueberries, to serve

Medium saucepan on a high heat | Kettle boiled | Heatproof bowl | Electric beater

Pour hot water into the pan until it's about 3cm deep and bring to the boil | Reduce the heat to a simmer | Put a heatproof bowl on top of the pan, ensuring the water doesn't touch the bottom | Break 85g of the dark chocolate into the bowl and leave it to melt | Remove and leave to cool a little

Pour the aquafaba into a large bowl and use the electric beater (a hand whisk won't cut it this time) to whisk the liquid for 10–15 minutes – it will gradually firm up, as if by magic | Stop when the mixture makes stiff peaks if you lift out the beaters | Gently fold in the melted chocolate, sugar, vanilla and salt using a large metal spoon or spatula, making sure you don't beat out too much air

Spoon the mousse into serving glasses or bowls and chill for 2 hours

Grate the remaining 15g chocolate | Dress the individual mousses with a handful of blueberries and a touch of grated chocolate just before serving

STICKY TOFFEE PUDDING

It's hard to describe just how good this dish is. You have to try it. It's just like Grandma used to make: incredibly smoky and toffee-and-caramel-flavoured. The notes of cinnamon, ginger and nutmeg add hints of deliciousness to the orgy of richness. This dish goes really well with a serving of dairy-free ice cream!

SERVES 6

170g dates
350ml plant-based milk
1 tsp vanilla extract
1½ tsp bicarbonate of soda
215g dairy-free butter
200g dark brown sugar
180g self-raising flour
½ tsp ground nutmeg
1 tsp ground ginger
1 tsp ground cinnamon
1 tsp salt
1 tbsp golden syrup
3 tbsp coconut cream

Preheat oven to 160°C | Small saucepan on a medium heat | 25 x 15 x 5cm ovenproof dish greased with dairy-free butter

Cut the dates into small pieces, removing the stones as you go | Put them in the saucepan along with the plant-based milk and vanilla extract and cook until the dates are soft, about 10 minutes

Take the pan off the heat and stir in the bicarbonate of soda | Let the liquid cool to room temperature | Add 115g of the dairy-free butter and 100g of the sugar | Add the flour, nutmeg, ginger, cinnamon and salt, and stir them through a few times with a spoon until just combined, but not overmixed

Pour the mixture into the greased baking dish, put the dish in the oven and bake for 35–40 minutes, until risen and a skewer inserted into the centre of the sponge comes out clean

Meanwhile, clean the saucepan and put it back on a medium heat | Put the golden syrup, the remaining 100g brown sugar and the remaining 100g dairy-free butter into the pan, stir and reduce the heat to low | Cook for 5 minutes until you have a syrup | Remove the pan from the hob, allow it to cool slightly and then stir in the coconut cream | Pour into a small jug

To serve, use a knife to cut the sticky toffee pudding into slices | Place each slice into a bowl and cover with the delicious toffee drizzle | Serve and enjoy!

MIXED BERRY CRUMBLE

This crumble is luxuriously fruity, crumbly and crunchy.
It's easy to make and great to share, perfect for a cool-
season dessert. You can, of course, use any berries that are
in season for this; we've opted for a mixed berry selection.
A little dairy-free oat cream or custard would work perfectly
with this dessert.

SERVES 6 – 8

1kg mixed berries, such as
   blackberries, raspberries,
   strawberries and blueberries
230g caster sugar
1 tsp vanilla extract
3 tbsp cornflour
230g wholemeal flour
230g rolled oats
1 tsp ground cinnamon
230g dairy-free butter or spread
dairy-free custard or oat cream,
   to serve, optional

Preheat oven to 180°C | 30 x 20cm baking dish

Put the berries, 100g of the sugar, the vanilla extract and cornflour into a large mixing bowl and mix together, making sure all the fruit is covered in the sugar and cornflour | Tip into the baking dish and smooth the top with the back of a spoon

Place the flour, oats and cinnamon in a bowl and mix well | Scoop small pieces of the dairy-free butter into the bowl with a spoon and then get your hands in and pinch and rub everything together with your fingertips until it looks like breadcrumbs | Add the remaining 130g sugar and mix well | Scatter the crumble mixture evenly all over the berry filling, covering it all the way to the edges

Put the dish in the hot oven and bake for 50 minutes, or until the top is golden and the fruit is bubbling up around the edges of the dish | Take out of the oven and serve with the dairy-free custard or oat cream, if you like

SALTED CARAMEL CHOCOLATE CRUNCH TART

Oozing with sugary, crunchy, caramel, chocolatey goodness, this insanely tasty dish has everything you could want from a dessert. It is regularly showcased at events since we're so proud of it, and it's got that 'pick-up-and-go' factor, so would sit comfortably in a buffet. This is the dish you'll want to make again and again.

SERVES 10

1 x packet ready-rolled dairy-free shortcrust pastry
160g coconut cream
200g light brown sugar
2 tsp sea salt
200g hazelnuts
100g pecans
100g dark chocolate
2 tsp vanilla extract

Preheat oven to 180°C | Line a small baking tray with parchment paper | Medium saucepan

Unroll the pastry on to the lined baking tray, making sure the edges of the pastry fold up the sides of the tray and pressing it into the corners | Chill in the freezer for 10 minutes to stop the pastry from shrinking and the sides from collapsing

Put the pastry in the hot oven and bake for about 30 minutes, or until golden brown (it will bubble a bit but don't worry, those bubbles will deflate | Take the tray out of the oven

Meanwhile, put the saucepan on a medium heat | Pour in the coconut cream and stir so that it becomes completely liquid | Pour in the sugar and stir continuously for at least 5 minutes, until the mixture thickens and darkens in colour | Sprinkle in the salt and stir it into the caramel

Put the hazelnuts and pecans into a mortar and break them up with the pestle (or put them in a plastic bag and bash them with a rolling pin) | Tip the broken nuts into the pan and stir them in so that they're well covered in the sticky caramel sauce | Break the chocolate into the pan and stir until it has melted into the caramel and the nuts are completely covered | Take the pan off the heat, stir in the vanilla extract and set aside

Pour the chocolate caramel into the pastry base and spread it out to the edges | Smooth the top with a spatula or smooth knife | Put the tart back in the oven for 3 minutes, then take it out and let it cool to room temperature in the tin | Put the cooled tart in the fridge for 30 minutes to cool down and firm up

Take the tart out of the fridge and carefully remove it from the tin | Cut into slices and serve

APPLE PEAR PIE

Who doesn't like a slice of warm apple pie? The cinnamon and apple flavours go together perfectly and complement the contrasting crispy crust and sweet, fruity centre. This one's pretty easy to prepare, made much easier by using ready-made shortcrust pastry. Everyone should have a good apple pie in their repertoire. This can be yours!

SERVES 6

1 x 500g block ready-made
   dairy-free shortcrust pastry
800g apples
500g pears
½ lemon
40g caster sugar
2 tbsp maple syrup
2 tsp ground cinnamon
2 tbsp flour
small pinch of salt
2 tbsp plant-based milk
1 tbsp brown sugar
soy cream, optional, to serve

Preheat oven to 180°C | Heavy baking sheet in oven | Clean work surface dusted liberally with flour | Rolling pin (or use a clean, dry wine bottle) | Board dusted with flour | Clear some space in the fridge | 23cm deep tart or pie tin | Pastry brush

Put the pastry on the floured work surface and roll it out to a rough rectangle about 3mm thick (about the thickness of a £1 coin) and wider than your pie tin | Lay the tin at one end of the pastry and cut around the base with a sharp knife to make a disc (this will be your lid) | Lay the rest of the pastry inside the pie tin | Press it neatly into the edges and all the way up the sides, making sure there's no trapped air | Cut away the excess pastry and use pieces to patch up any gaps | Lay the pastry lid and any excess on the floured board

Put the tin in the fridge for 15 minutes to chill along with the pastry on the board (this will stop it shrinking in the oven)

Meanwhile, peel and core the apples and pears and cut them roughly into 1cm chunks | Put them in a large bowl and squeeze over the juice of the lemon, catching any pips in your other hand | Add the caster sugar, maple syrup, cinnamon, flour and salt and mix together with a wooden spoon

Spread the apple mixture evenly into the chilled pie base | Lay the lid over the top and crimp the edges by pinching all around the rim between your thumb and forefinger, or by squashing the lid and sides together with a fork | Cut off any excess pastry with a sharp knife

Use any leftover pastry to make decorations for the top of the pie (leaves, flowers, BOSH! letters etc.) | Brush the bottoms of the pastry shapes with a little of the plant-based milk and gently press them on to the pie lid to secure

Put the tin on top of the hot baking sheet in the oven and bake for 40 minutes, then take it out of the oven | Brush the pie with the remaining plant-based milk, sprinkle it with brown sugar and put it back in the oven for 10–12 minutes, or until it's crisp and golden on top

Take the pie out of the oven | Let it cool down for at least 15 minutes before serving with soy cream, if using

08

BREAKFASTS

From daily smoothies
To weekly bowls of goodness
Start your day right here

BANANA PANCAKES

We had to include some banana pancakes! This is a wonderful easy-to-prepare breakfast for those mornings when you are looking for something delicious and impressive to start your day. Experiment with toppings, but if you make sure there is plenty of fruit it counts as one of your five (or ten) a day!

SERVES 2

1½ ripe bananas
½ tbsp coconut oil, plus extra for frying
½ tsp ground cinnamon
90g plain flour
15g caster sugar
1 tsp baking powder
240ml plant-based milk
30g pecans
50ml maple syrup
20g dark chocolate

Preheat oven to 50°C | Ovenproof plate | Food processor | Frying pan on a medium-high heat

Put one banana, the coconut oil, cinnamon, flour, sugar, baking powder and plant-based milk into the food processor and whizz to a smooth batter | Add a little coconut oil to the frying pan and warm it so that it's reasonably hot, but not smoking

Pour about 3 tablespoons of the mixture for each pancake you can fit into the pan and fry for about 2 minutes, until bubbles start to appear on the surface of the pancakes | Flip them over and fry the other sides for another 1–2 minutes | Remove to the ovenproof plate and put it in the oven to keep warm while you cook the rest of the pancakes

Slice the ½ banana | Put the pecans in a mortar and lightly crush with a pestle (or put them in a plastic bag and crush with a rolling pin)

Stack the pancakes on 2 serving plates | Put the banana slices on top and scatter over the pecans | Drizzle with lashings of maple syrup and grate over the chocolate

CHOCOLATE GRANOLA

Remember how chocolate cereal used to make the milk go chocolatey? Well this incredibly moreish dish has that in abundance. It makes a fantastic breakfast, but would also work as a replacement for popcorn on movie night. For a healthier (but still tasty) version, remove the sugar.

SERVES 6–8

60g Brazil nuts
60g pecan nuts
60g hazelnuts
75g coconut flakes
½ tsp sea salt
300g oats
50g coconut sugar
150g coconut oil
25ml maple syrup
1 tsp vanilla extract
50g dark chocolate
50g raisins

Preheat oven to 140°C | Line a large baking tray | Large saucepan on a very low heat

Put all the nuts in the middle of a clean tea towel, wrap them up and break them with a rolling pin so that they are about the size of raisins | Tip the broken nuts into a mixing bowl | Add the coconut flakes, salt, oats and coconut sugar and mix everything together with a wooden spoon

Slowly melt the coconut oil in the saucepan | Add the maple syrup and vanilla extract and mix everything together | Pour the dry ingredients from the bowl into the saucepan and mix it all together

Pour the granola on to the lined baking tray (the wider the tray, the crunchier the granola) | Put the tray in the oven and bake for 40 minutes

Take the tray out of the oven | Break the dark chocolate into small, chocolate-chip-sized chunks and sprinkle them over the granola along with the raisins | Leave to cool to room temperature

Break up the granola into bite-sized chunks and transfer to an airtight container | Enjoy your delicious granola with lashings of plant-based milk and chopped fresh fruit

BOSH! BREAKFAST TOASTS

The humble slice of bread, toasted to perfection, is a mighty meal to behold. Here are three of our favourite ways to enjoy a quick-fix mini English breakfast. They're most delicious with quality sourdough bread that brings additional flavour to the meal, even better if it's from a real baker! The better the bread, the better the breakfast.

CREAMY GARLIC MUSHROOM TOAST

So. Rich. So Creamy. Cannot. Compute. This garlicky mushroom dish is effortless and full of voluptuous, creamy flavours.

SERVES 2

Large frying pan on a medium-high heat | Toaster or grill

350g mushrooms
2 small garlic cloves
2 spring onions
1 tbsp olive oil
2 large or 4 small slices
   good-quality fresh bread
1½ tbsp dairy-free butter,
   plus extra for spreading
75ml soy cream
small handful fresh parsley leaves
salt and black pepper

Slice the mushrooms | Peel and mince the garlic | Trim the roots and ends from the spring onions and finely slice

Put the olive oil in the pan | Add the mushrooms and cook for 10 minutes | Add the garlic and three-quarters of the spring onions (saving some of the green ends for garnish) | Cook for a further 3 minutes

Put the bread in the toaster or under the grill

Add the dairy-free butter to the pan of mushrooms and stir it through until it melts | Pour the soy cream into the pan and stir it into the mushrooms | Take the pan off the heat | Season to taste with salt and pepper

Roughly chop the parsley and stir most of it through the mushrooms | Take the toast out of the toaster or grill and spread it with dairy-free butter | Divide the mushroom mixture equally between the toasts | Sprinkle over the remaining spring onions and parsley | Grind over a little black pepper and serve immediately

SMOKY BBQ BEANS ON TOAST

These home-made BBQ beans are a revelation. They're smoky, rich and incredibly punchy, plus they're filled with protein. Feel free to adjust the chilli to suit your taste.

SERVES 2

½ onion
2 garlic cloves
1 tbsp olive oil
1 tbsp tomato purée
¼ tsp smoked paprika
¼ tsp chilli powder
¼ tsp dried thyme
1 tbsp light brown sugar
1 tbsp light soy sauce
1 x 400g tin cannellini beans
2 large or 4 small slices
    good-quality fresh bread
100g passata
dairy-free butter, for spreading
fresh parsley leaves, to garnish,
    optional
salt and black pepper

Medium saucepan on a medium heat | Toaster or grill

Peel and finely chop the onion and garlic | Add the olive oil to the pan | Add the onion and garlic and stir until the onion is translucent and soft, about 10 minutes

Add the tomato purée, smoked paprika, chilli powder, thyme, sugar and soy sauce and stir them into the onions | Cook for a further 2 minutes

Drain and rinse the cannellini beans, then add them to the pan | Stir them around so that they're covered in the sauce | Cook for another 2–3 minutes

Put the bread in the toaster or under the grill

Pour the passata into the pan and let it simmer until the sauce has thickened, about 5 minutes | Chop the parsley, if using

Taste the sauce and season it with pepper and a little salt | Take the toast out of the toaster or grill and spread it with dairy-free butter | Put the beans on top, sprinkle over the parsley, if using, and serve immediately

TOFU SCRAMBLE ON TOAST

This version of the classic scramble uses tofu as a base and is spongy, crumbly and super satisfying. Added to our Big Breakfast (see page 265) it would create a meal for a king and queen.

SERVES 2

½ small red onion
1 garlic clove
50g baby leaf spinach
2 tbsp olive oil
1 x 280g block extra-firm tofu
2 tsp dairy-free butter,
    plus more for spreading
1 tbsp nutritional yeast
1 tsp ground turmeric
½ tsp chilli flakes
2 large or 4 small slices
    good-quality fresh bread
salt and black pepper

Large frying pan on a medium heat | Toaster or grill

Peel and finely slice the onion and garlic | Roughly chop the spinach

Add the olive oil to the pan | Add the onions and garlic and cook until the onions are well softened, about 10 minutes | Crumble the tofu into the pan along with the 2 teaspoons of dairy-free butter | Add the nutritional yeast, turmeric and chilli flakes and stir everything together | Cook for around 5 minutes | Season with salt and pepper

Put the bread in the toaster or under the grill

Add the spinach to the pan and stir until well wilted, another 1–2 minutes | Taste again and season if necessary

Take the toast out of the toaster or grill and spread it with dairy-free butter | Top it with the spinach and scramble, grind over some black pepper and serve immediately

BANANA BREAD

Is it a dessert? Is it a breakfast? We can't decide. Is it tasty? Hell yes. Want to know what makes this amazing recipe even better? Spread some peanut butter on top. Oh my goodness it's insane. Or dairy-free ice cream to turn it into a whopper of a dessert.

250g plain flour
75g light brown sugar
75g white sugar
1½ tbsp cocoa powder
½ tsp bicarbonate of soda
½ tsp salt
½ tsp ground allspice
110g dairy-free butter
3 ripe bananas
60ml almond milk
2 tbsp maple syrup
1 tsp apple cider vinegar
1 tsp vanilla extract
60g dark chocolate
50g pecans

Preheat oven to 170°C | Line a 1kg loaf tin with parchment paper | Food processor

Pour all the ingredients except the dark chocolate and pecans into the food processor and whizz them to a thick mixture | Take out the blade and scrape any excess mixture back into the bowl

Break the dark chocolate and pecans into small pieces and tip them into the bowl | Mix everything together

Pour the mixture into the lined loaf tin and put it in the oven | Bake for 60–65 minutes, or until a skewer inserted into the middle of the loaf comes out clean | Take the tin out of the oven and leave the bread to cool to room temperature | Remove the bread from the tin and cut it into slices to serve

THE BIG BREAKFAST

The only way to deal with a big day ahead is to start with a breakfast of champions. This is a big, filling breakfast that's relatively healthy, best enjoyed with friends. Serve with your sauce of choice and a strong cup of tea or coffee. Feel free to freestyle this one, adding little extras like scrambled tofu (see page 261), hummus, fried potatoes or fried bread.

SERVES 2

1 x portion Hash Browns ingredients
   (see page 267)
4 frozen vegan sausages
1 x portion Basil Tomatoes ingredients
   (see page 266)
1 x portion Herb Mushrooms ingredients
   (see page 266)
200g tinned baked beans
1 avocado
2 slices bread
dairy-free butter, for spreading
tomato ketchup or brown sauce, to serve
salt and black pepper

Preheat oven to 180°C | Line 2 baking trays | 2 small saucepans, one with a lid, both on a medium heat | Frying pan on a medium heat | Toaster or grill

Timing is everything with this one; follow these instructions and you can't go far wrong

First make the Hash Browns following the instructions on page 267, and put them on a baking tray | Put the sausages on the same tray as the hash browns | Put the tray in the oven and cook for 20–25 minutes

Make the Basil Tomatoes in the small saucepan with a lid, following the instructions on page 266, and leave them warming on a low-medium heat, stirring occasionally

Make the Herb Mushrooms in the frying pan, following the instructions on page 266 and leave them warming on a low-medium heat, stirring occasionally

Pour the baked beans into the second small saucepan and warm them, stirring occasionally.

Halve and carefully stone the avocado by tapping the stone firmly with the heel of a knife so that it lodges in the pit, then twist and remove the stone | Run a dessert spoon around the inside of the skin to scoop out the avocado halves, then slice finely | Sprinkle over a little salt and pepper

Toast the bread and spread with dairy-free butter | Spoon everything on to plates and serve with brown sauce or tomato ketchup

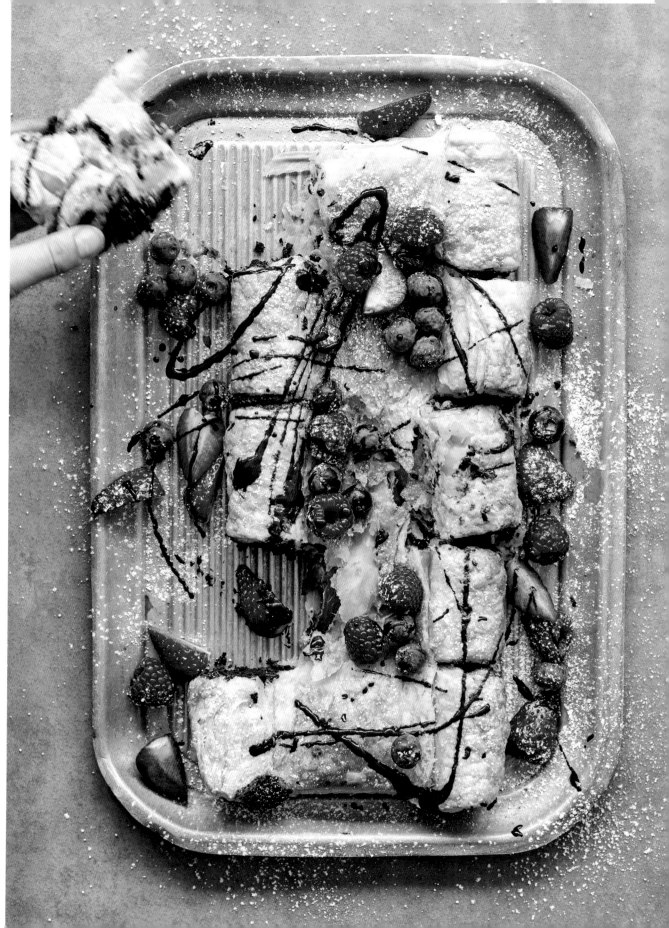

CHOCOLATE CROISSANT TEARER SHARER

This is an easy indulgence, created as a result of our love of pains au chocolat. The ready-rolled pastry makes it an effortless, deliciously moreish dish, perfect for the morning after. It's simple to make, impressive to look at (definitely put the fruity bits on top for added wow factor) and just that little bit naughty.

SERVES 4—6

100g dark chocolate
2½ tbsp icing sugar,
    plus extra for dusting
2 x sheets ready-rolled dairy-free
    puff pastry
2 tbsp plant-based milk
handful strawberries
handful blueberries
handful raspberries
oat or soy cream, to serve

Preheat oven to 180°C | Medium saucepan with 3cm water on a medium-low heat | Heatproof bowl | Line a large baking sheet with parchment paper | Pastry brush

Put the heatproof bowl on top of the saucepan, making sure the bottom of the bowl isn't touching the water, and reduce the heat to low | Break 75g of the chocolate into the bowl and stir occasionally with a wooden spoon until the chocolate has melted | Pour in the icing sugar, stir to mix it in completely without any lumps and take the pan off the heat

Lay 1 sheet of puff pastry on to the lined baking sheet | Pour most of the melted chocolate on to the centre of the pastry and spread it out, leaving a 2cm gap around the edges | Lay the second sheet of pastry flush on top (you may want to ask a friend for help) | Gently press the 2 sheets of pastry together all the way round the edges

With a sharp knife, make 5 evenly spaced cuts into the long edges of the pastry so that they reach about 5cm in from the edges | You should be left with a strip of pastry running down the middle of the sheets that is at least 3cm wide, with 5 flaps of pastry either side

Cut the remaining chocolate into 10 chunks and place 1 chunk in the middle of each flap of pastry | Roll the flaps over the chocolate chunks, taking care not to cover the middle section, and press them to seal in the chocolate | Brush all over the top with the plant-based milk | Put the baking sheet in the oven and bake for 30—35 minutes, until the pastry is golden and slightly crispy

Take the baking sheet out of the oven and scatter the fresh berries along the middle section | Drizzle over the remaining melted chocolate | Dust lightly with icing sugar and serve immediately with a little oat or soy cream on the side for people to pour over if they wish

SIMPLE JAPANESE BREAKFAST

We are huge fans of Japan and Japanese food. A common breakfast in Japan is a smorgasbord of small dishes that often includes miso soup and some rice. Combine these two simple ingredients with the deep umami-flavoured sesame cucumbers, and you have a delicious breakfast that can be whipped together really quickly. This will set you up for an awesome day. Turn the page to see it in all its glory!

SERVES 2

1 x portion Perfectly Boiled Rice
   (see page 207) or 1 x packet
   pre-cooked basmati rice
½ x jar pickled ginger
Japanese Pickle (see opposite)
2 x sachets vegetarian miso soup
sesame seeds, for sprinkling
small handful coriander, to serve
wasabi, to serve
sriracha sauce, to serve

FOR THE SESAME CUCUMBERS
1 large cucumber
1 fresh red chilli
4 tbsp sesame oil
2 tbsp soy sauce
1 tsp rice wine vinegar

Small saucepan with a lid on a high heat | Chopsticks | Large frying pan

Tip the pre-cooked rice into a mixing bowl, fluff it with a fork and transfer to a serving bowl

Slice the cucumber in half from top to bottom | Take one half and lay it skin side up on a chopping board | Place a chopstick on either side of the cucumber | Take a sharp knife and cut diagonal slices all the way along the cucumber as finely as you can (the chopsticks will ensure you don't cut all the way through) | Take the chopsticks away and cut the cucumber into 6 equal pieces | Repeat with the other half of the cucumber

Rip the stem from the chilli, cut it in half lengthways and remove the seeds, if you prefer a milder flavour, and roughly chop

Put the large frying pan on a high heat and add the sesame oil | Add the chilli to the pan and fry for 90 seconds | Add the soy sauce and rice wine vinegar | Add the cucumber and fry for 2–3 minutes, until softened but not browned, turning the pieces a couple of times | Remove the cucumber from the pan with a slotted spoon and leave the sauce to bubble for a further minute, until slightly thickened

Spoon some rice on to each serving plate | Place a handful of pickled ginger and a tablespoon of Japanese pickle on to each plate | Empty the sachets of miso soup into 2 mugs or miso soup bowls, pour over freshly boiled water and stir

Divide the cucumber between the plates and pour some of the cooking liquid over the rice | Sprinkle over some sesame seeds and fresh coriander and place a dab of wasabi and sriracha on to each plate | Serve with the miso soup alongside and enjoy an incredibly easy, healthy and fresh-feeling start to the day!

JAPANESE PICKLE

You might need to find a Chinese supermarket to get hold of daikon, or you can order it online. This is best after one or two days in the fridge, but you can eat it after a couple of hours. Use as an accompaniment to any Asian-influenced meal.

MAKES 850G

1 large daikon (about 350g)
1 tbsp salt
2cm piece fresh ginger
120ml water
100g sugar
120ml rice wine vinegar
1 tsp ground turmeric

2–3 x 500g jars with lids | Medium saucepan

First, sterilise your jars and lids by washing them in hot, soapy water and then filling them to the top with boiling water | Drain on a clean tea towel until completely dry

Peel the daikon and thinly slice using a mandolin or vegetable peeler (or a very sharp knife) | Put the slices into a colander, scatter over the salt, toss to coat and leave for 30 minutes

Meanwhile, peel the ginger by scraping off the skin with a spoon and cut it into very fine matchsticks

Put the pan on a medium heat | Pour in the water and sugar and stir to dissolve the sugar | Bring to the boil | Add the vinegar, turmeric and ginger | Turn down the heat slightly and leave to simmer for 2–3 minutes | Remove from the heat and leave to cool

Squeeze the daikon with the back of a spoon to remove as much liquid as possible | Divide it between the sterilised jars and pour over the pickling liquid | Put the lids on, put them in the fridge and leave to pickle away | This can be stored in the fridge for 3 months

BREAKFAST SMOOTHIES

Putting a load of healthy things in a smoothie is a great way, if not the best way, to start the day. It's quick, easy and mess free and gives you the feeling that you are already winning the day. These are three of our favourite smoothies.

To make smoothies a part of your daily routine, simply keep a store of fruit and veg in the freezer and blend it up regularly to keep your fruit and veg varied and get a healthy mix of goodness in your body.

TURMERIC
POWERSHOT

TURMERIC POWERSHOT

Be warned, this is one powerful get-you-out-of-bed drink. This will get you and your immune system up with a kick, and gives a noticeable, immediate hit of caffeine-free alertness. It's not for the faint-hearted, but it's very good for you. If you want to turn this into a spicy 'Smoochie' cocktail, pour a shot of vodka into each glass.

MAKES 6 SMALL GLASSES

Liquidiser

2 Braeburn apples
2 oranges
1 lemon
6cm piece fresh ginger
1½ tsp ground turmeric
½ tsp cayenne pepper
100ml water

Core the apples and chop them into pieces | Peel the oranges and lemon and separate the segments | Peel the ginger by scraping off the skin with a spoon and roughly chop | Put all the ingredients into the liquidiser and whizz for a few minutes until you have a thick, liquidy paste

Strain the mixture into a large jug through a sieve, pressing out as much of the liquid as possible and discard the pulp | Pour into glasses and serve

CHOCONANA PROTEIN SHAKE

Who doesn't want to drink a healthy chocolate milkshake for breakfast? This one's choc-full of protein and will give you a great boost for the day ahead.

MAKES 2–4 GLASSES

Liquidiser

2 bananas (fresh or frozen for a cooler smoothie)
70g rolled oats
3 tbsp smooth peanut butter
2 tbsp cacao powder
2 tbsp vegan protein powder, optional
400ml plant-based milk
100ml coconut water
1 tsp maple syrup

Put all the ingredients into the liquidiser and whizz to a thick milkshake | Pour into glasses and serve

GREEN GOODNESS

Inspired by Rhonda Patrick's super-green morning smoothie, this is filled with lots of the vitamins and nutrients your body needs to survive and recover. Be warned, this one is health first, taste second, but drink it regularly and you'll feel like a superhero.

SERVES 2

50g kale
50g spinach
50g chard
8 blueberries
250ml water
½ avocado
½ banana
½ apple
2 cherry tomatoes
1 tbsp peanut butter

Liquidiser

Put the kale, spinach, chard and blueberries and 50ml of the water into a liquidiser and whizz for 1–2 minutes until you have a smooth paste

Scoop the flesh of the avocado half into the liquidiser | Add the banana, apple, cherry tomatoes, peanut butter and the remaining 200ml of water | Blitz until you have a thick and creamy smoothie (if you prefer it a little thinner, add a bit more water) | Drink and feel healthier all day long

Nutrition

Eating a plant-based, vegan diet is one of the healthiest things you can do for your body. Plus, it feels fantastic. So where do we get our protein from? Plants!

It's a myth that you need animal flesh to get protein. There are world-class athletes who are thriving on a plant-based diet and the strongest animals in the world get their protein from plants. We get ours from nuts and seeds, grains, tofu, beans and peas and other veggies, both in their natural forms and prepared in things like peanut butter, hummus and even seitan, a meat substitute made from wheat gluten.

You can get all the essential amino acids from plants, but you do need to eat a variety. Some protein-rich foods, such as amaranth, quinoa, cacao and hemp, contain all the vital amino acids, just like meat does. But even the plant foods that don't contain all the amino acids can be combined to give you all the essential amino acids. For example, peanut butter on toast or rice and peas are both complete sources of protein. Boom!

In our opinion, a whole food plant-based diet is a really healthy way to live your life. It doesn't include too much oil or refined carbohydrate, however, we operate on an 80/20 principle (thanks, Derek Sarno, for this one) where 80% of the time we eat tasty but healthy food and 20% of the time we treat ourselves.

It's important to realise that we are not simply talking about a typical diet with the meat and dairy removed. We eat a different food pyramid entirely, one which involves loads of delicious fruit, veggies, nuts, seeds and grains. And if you're eating them in a variety of colours, especially dark green, then you are likely to be getting all the nutrients you need. Opposite you'll find a handy guide on how to get the nutrients that every human needs, be they meat-eater, vegetarian or vegan.

Good sources of protein

Legumes
- Black beans
- Broad beans
- Cannellini beans
- Kidney beans
- Pinto beans
- Haricot beans
- Soy beans/Edamame
- Green beans
- Chickpeas
- Garden peas
- Lentils
- Tempeh
- Tofu

Grains
- Brown rice
- Buckwheat
- Bulgur wheat
- Corn
- Oats
- Quinoa
- Seitan
- Soba noodles
- Wholegrain bread

Nuts
- Almond
- Brazil
- Cashew
- Hazelnut
- Macadamia
- Peanuts
- Pecan
- Walnut

Seeds
- Chia
- Flax
- Hemp
- Pumpkin
- Sesame
- Sunflower

Vegetables
- Artichoke
- Asparagus
- Avocado
- Broccoli
- Brussels sprouts
- Kale
- Mushrooms
- Potatoes
- Spinach
- Spring greens
- Sweetcorn

Spreads
- Hummus and tahini
- Nut butter

Other
- Dark chocolate
- Goji berries
- Nutritional yeast
- Plant-based cheese
- Spirulina

Calcium

Strengthens bones and teeth, helps blood to clot, aids brain function and helps muscles to contract.

- Non-dairy fortified milks and yoghurts
- Tofu
- Almonds
- Brazil nuts
- Chickpeas
- Curly kale
- Pak choi
- Spring greens
- Watercress
- Figs
- Oranges

Vitamin A

Helps your body's immune system to work properly. Aids vision in dim light. Keeps skin and the lining of some parts of the body, such as the nose, healthy.

- Butternut squash
- Cantaloupe
- Carrots and carrot juice
- Kale
- Pumpkin
- Spinach
- Sweet potatoes
- Supplements

Vitamin D

Helps keep bones, teeth and muscles healthy. Plays an important role in cancer prevention, mental health and bone protection.

- Fortified cereals, soya products and spreads
- Sunshine! Make sure you get out in the sun for 10 minutes every day
- Supplements, if necessary

Iodine

Important for normal functioning and growth of the body. Plays an important role in the functioning of the thyroid gland.

- Fortified almond, soy, oat, hemp milk
- Kelp, seaweed, nori and sea vegetables
- Iodine supplements

Magnesium

Essential for hundreds of reactions in your body, such as repairing and regenerating cells and providing energy, so don't be deficient! It's found in chlorophyll (found in green plants) so eat loads of green!

- Avocados
- Chard
- Spinach
- Black beans
- Bananas
- Figs
- Almonds
- Pumpkin seeds
- Dark chocolate

Zinc

Helps regulate and improve functioning of the immune system.

- Leafy green vegetables
- Legumes
- Sprouted seeds and beans
- Nuts
- Seeds
- Oats

Vitamin B12

Helps maintain nerve cells, including those in the brain. It helps your mood, energy, heart, digestion and more. Vitamin B12 isn't found naturally in plants, but you can get yours from loads of other sources.

- B12 supplements
- Fortified cereals and non-dairy milks
- Fortified fruit and vegetable juices
- Nutritional yeast
- Yeast extract (e.g. Marmite or Vegemite)

Iron

Essential for good metabolism, healthy blood flow and therefore oxygenation of the body. Improves muscle and brain function.

- Artichokes
- Dark green leafy veg
- Sweet potatoes
- Beans
- Chickpeas and tahini
- Garden peas
- Lentils
- Cashews
- Pistachios
- Pumpkin, pumpkin seeds, and sesame seeds
- Dried fruit (e.g. dates, figs, prunes and apricots)
- Tofu
- Dark chocolate

Omega 3

Important for proper brain function and maintaining a healthy cardiovascular system.

- Chia seeds
- Ground flaxseed (linseed)
- Hemp seeds
- Walnuts and walnut oil
- Flaxseed, rapeseed and hempseed oils
- Algae-based supplements

Fibre

Helps the body's digestive system, promotes a healthy biome (your gut bacteria), and helps you regulate your weight.

- Baked potato (with skin)
- Beans
- Berries
- Bran cereal
- Brown rice
- Nuts and seeds
- Oatmeal
- Popcorn
- Vegetables (the crunchier the better)
- Whole grains, whole grain bread, whole grain pasta etc.

Thanks

First and foremost we would like to thank YOU for reading this book. We hope you love it, and that you find your new favourite recipe in here.

Second and of equal importance, we want to thank every one of our fans. Every single person who has ever watched, shared, liked or commented on one of our recipes. Thanks so much for being part of the BOSH! journey. We love you all!

We would like to thank Lisa Milton, Rachel Kenny, Louise McGrory, Sarah Hammond, JP, Georgina Green, Darren Shoffren, Ben North, Sophie Calder, Alison Lindsay, Bengono Bessala and all the great people at HQ and HarperCollins who have embraced us with open arms and embarked on a huge journey with us. Liate Stehlik, Lynn Grady, Cassie Jones, Kaitlin Harri, Anwesha Basu, Kara Zauberman, Tavia Kowalchuk at William Morrow. Whatever you would do, or dream you can, begin it. Boldness has genius, power and magic in it. Lizzie Mayson, Pip Spence and Sarah Birks for creating seriously amazing works of art out of our recipes, and for having such a fun month with us along with Steph McLeod, Josh Payne, Clare Gray, Esther Clark, Nicola Roberts and Amy Stephenson. Paul Palmer-Edwards at Grade for the book design and the patience. Also, Caroline McArthur, Helena Caldon, Jenna Leiter, Katy Gilhooly and Jordan Bourke. Dr Rupy Aujla at The Doctor's Kitchen for some badass nutrition tips.

Rachel, Mary, Georgie, Sophie, Blaise, Gemma, Lucy, Avril and everyone at James Grant for seeing the potential and jumping on board, then helping us grow, grow and grow. Megan, Becky and Sarah and all at Carver PR for all their great work, and the fun we've had together!

Cathy, for being a badass with a camera and a machine, a badass cook and true friend. Bonita, Beverley and all those who helped out as part of the BOSH! team for bringing such great work to the world and helping us test our recipes again and again and again. Sarah Durber, for your ongoing hustle and ability to help us get shit done. This book is here thanks to your badassness.

Jamie, Paul, Henry, Mitch, Molly, Joe, Stefane, Chris, Bamber, Teej, Lewis, Sami, Chan, Adam, Raman and every other world-class human at Jungle Creations for supporting us thus far. You guys rock. Pasa, the absolute legend, for all the fun of Pashover and the important introductions you continue to make. Luke Robinson, chef extraordinaire, for being a culinary wizard, an inspiration and for your help kicking off BOSH! with a bang. Dawn Carr for being a badass. James Heaphy and Oli for finding the time to nail our first few shoots with awesome footage (in between cigarette breaks).

Adam Biddle, for introducing Ian and me to the benefits of plant-based vegan food, the myths surrounding protein and the wonders of the black. Tim Stillwell at Burrito Kitchen for the giggles. Natalie and everyone at the Good agency for your badass brains. Taimi for your wonderful designs, your incredible work and your altruistic spirit.

All the people in our world who are striving to make positive changes. There are so many, but for those who have made a difference in our lives: Damien Clarkson and Judy Nadel at Vevolution, Matthew Glover and Jane Land at Veganuary, James Aspey, Serena @vegansofldn, Ellie @kindstateofmind, Robbie and Klaus at @plantbasednews, everyone at Mercy4Animals, PETA, Kate and the whole team at Animal Equality. Harriet Emily for THAT chocolate cake.

Tommy Marshall (Third Person Lurkin), Derek Sarno, Tim Shieff, Grace Regan, Kate Werner, Morgan Masters, Deni Kirkova, Louis Buck, Nicky Johnston, Danny Howells and Rachel Smith.

IAN THEASBY

Henry, for your unwavering friendship, insane drive and faith in me. Mum, Dad and Frances, for the constant love and support – thank you. Alex, for being there every step of the way. Tom, for being a real level-headed force. Jenny, for your unrivalled and infectious positivity. Kweku, you're a don mega. Joe, for all those late-night chats. Mase, for knowing exactly what the dilly be.

Zulf, your wise words always resonate. CB, for being the ultimate yeah yeah yeah man. Addison, you're one of God's finest. Ben, for being the best rapper alive. Molly, you gave me more drive than you'll ever know. Prosecco Club, stand up! All the London crew for your love and loyalty – you know who you are. And all the Sheffield crew for being there since day one.

HENRY FIRTH

Ian, for your friendship, creativity, work ethic and patience. Emily-Jane Williams, for being a true worldy and inspiration. Jamie Bolding, for being a hustler, a friend and a driving force in the world. Jane, Mark, Alice and Graham for being awesome. Michael, Bruce, Jean, Gus, Arthur, Nick, Sukey, Alison, Curtis, Claire, Nick and all my family, for their love and support. Kweku, for your expert advice and fun times. Alex for two years on the ship.

Alex and Catherine, for being awesome. Nat and Khairan, for being the coolest people I know. Duncan and Martha plus Ernie, for making me cry. Tim and Susie, for pushing the bunny to the front of Wren's pram. Addison and Claire. Josh, Charlotte and Leo. Ekow, Claire and Hugo. Marcus, Ellie and Jasper. JP, Alex, Anna, Ellie, Taz, Bev and all the Allplants crew for all the love and support during the early days of BOSH!

INDEX